Math Dance

with Dr. Schaffer and Mr. Stern

Whole-Body Math and Movement Activities
for the K-12 Classroom

By Karl Schaffer, Erik Stern, and Scott Kim

Published by MoveSpeakSpin
P.O. Box 8055
Santa Cruz, CA 95061

Dedication
This book is dedicated to all those students, young and old,
who cannot but move when they think, and think when they move.

First printing: November 26, 2001.
This printing November, 2016
If you try the activities in this book, let us know what works, what doesn't, and how to improve it. Please send comments to:

Karl Schaffer	karl_schaffer@yahoo.com	831-335-1861
Erik Stern	estern@weber.edu	801-626-6615
Scott Kim	scott@shufflebrain.com	

Or visit us on the web at: http://www.mathdance.org

Copyright
© 2001 Karl Schaffer, Erik Stern, Scott Kim. All rights reserved.
Published by MoveSpeakSpin, POB 8055, Santa Cruz, CA 95061
ISBN-13: 978-0615728186
ISBN-10: 0615728189

Reproduction
No part of this book may be reproduced by any mechanical, photographic, or electronic process, or in the form of a phonograph recording, nor may it be stored in a retrieval system, transmitted, or otherwise copied for public or private use, without written permission from the publisher. Individual teachers who have purchased the book for use in their own classrooms may freely copy the blackline masters for use in their classes.

Art credits
Graphic and cover design by Scott Kim
Illustrations by Scott Kim & Karl Schaffer
Photography by:
Ronn Reinberg: front cover lower left & lower right, 7 right, 66, 77 left, 104, 116
Dorah Rosen: 77 right, 85, 89, 106, 107, 112, 115
Utah photographer: front cover top right, 23, 25, 44, 45, 46
Steve Savage: front cover middle left, 5, 131
Hazen Imaging: 16, 79, 80, 81, back cover
Willow Run Middle School (Ann Arbor): front cover top left
John Bakalis: 7 left
Karl Schaffer: 10
Clark Taylor: 98

Table of Contents

Preface — *4*

Introduction *5*

How to Use this Book — *10*

Chapter 1. **How Many Ways to Shake Hands?** — *16*
    A new look at an everyday gesture

Chapter 2. **Clap Your Name** — *23*
    Rhythmic sense and number sense

Chapter 3. **Heads or Tails** — *31*
    Understanding uncertainty through chance in dance

Chapter 4. **The Incredible Expanding Path** — *38*
    From lines on paper to paths in space

Chapter 5. **Threesies** — *44*
    An introduction to symmetry

Chapter 6. **Watch Your p's and q's** — *52*
    Moving through four types of symmetry

Chapter 7. **Twisted Addition** — *66*
    Combining one symmetry with another

Chapter 8. **Hand Figures** — *77*
    Making shapes with your hands, arms and body

Chapter 9. **Figures in String** — *85*
    Beyond cat's cradle into the third dimension

Chapter 10. **Stick Figures** — *98*
    Making large forms in space

Chapter 11. **Moving with Giant Tangrams** — *104*
    Geometric shapes dancing in space

Chapter 12. **Storytelling wth Giant Tangrams** — *112*
    Illustrating stories with geometric shapes

Chapter 13. **Staging a Show** — *119*

Chapter 14. **Assessment** — *123*

Math Dance Bibliography — *127*

About the Authors — *131*

Preface

This book is the product of over ten years of work. We are pleased to have it in the form you hold before you. Earlier versions of some of the chapters have been distributed in handout form, and we have countless versions of one- and two-page handouts that we have used in our various workshops. Six chapters have been available in a more rudimentary form on the web for the past year. The material included here is from those classes with which we have the most experience.

Many individuals have helped with comments, ideas, criticisms, and stories from the classroom. Eliz Laren helped with the initial workshops back in 1991. Patti Larrick, formerly of the Bay Area California Arts Project, hired us frequently to perform and teach in workshop settings. Sherry Fraser saw the first math dance performance while in rehearsal and immediately booked us as the opening event at a major conference of math teachers. Susanne Young, formerly with Young Audiences San Jose, saw the value in our work at an early stage, and helped us get going with our performing. Our long-time technical director Ronn Reinberg made the performances work, and their success always fueled our classroom work. Costumer Diane Neri Stern made sure we dressed for the occasion, and took care of Walker and Cole when we were off being math dancers. Lori Allen Siegelman, First Lady of Alabama and good friend, brought us to Montgomery twice to work for exciting residencies with the youth of Alabama. David Masunaga of Iolani School in Honolulu, has been an enthusiastic contributor to our residencies and ideas. Our administrative aides and board members over the years have borne our perennial disorganization in good humor: Sara Wilbourne, Gary Yamane, Shirlee Byrd, Rachel Hines, Amy Sugar, Virginia Wright, Leroy Clark, Terry Watson, Layne Goldman, Richard Polse and many others. Longtime company members Gregg Lizenbery and Chris Jones have been an integral part of the growth of our choreographic work, and so by association they have helped us in our math dance work. Thanks to Amy Jo Kim for supporting Scott in his efforts to finish this book. Mostly we would like to thank each other for the never-ending collaborative process of ideas, feedback, critiques, and discussions that have solidified our own understandings. Leslie Fisher helped proofread the manuscript. Any remaining mistakes are solely the responsibility of the authors.

Many acknowledgements should be made for the support, financial and critical, of this work. The National Endowment for the Arts provided funding for the years 1999–2002 for new choreographic work integrating mathematics and dance, for touring of that work in residencies that allow us take the ideas into the classroom, and also to support our continued work on creating and refining these teaching materials. This made it possible for the authors to gather in one location when the effort was needed. The California Arts Council has provided continuing support for the dance company within which we have done our joint creative work. The Cultural Council of Santa Cruz County and their Spectra program have, over the years, harbored some of our staunchest supporters, and provided funding for new math dance performances, which always seem to lead to new classroom ideas. The Djerassi Resident Arts Program gave us a one-month residency away from the workday world in the summer of 1999 during which we did major work on a new concert, and made significant progress on this book. Last, but not least, we thank the many individuals who have seen fit to lend financial support to our ongoing efforts to create dances and bring them to the public, and to encourage people to move and think in the classroom setting as well.

Introduction

In 1990 two of us (Karl Schaffer and Erik Stern) created our first math dance stage performance, *Dr. Schaffer and Mr. Stern: Two Guys Dancing about Math*. Since then the members of our dance company have developed five more math dance shows, performed for over a hundred thousand people, and taught workshops to hundreds of classes. Many teachers have written or spoken to us about the strengths and weaknesses of the particular activities and have helped us hone our methods. The ages and grade levels of participants in our workshops have run the gamut from kindergarten to college level math and dance classes, from teacher workshops to gatherings of artists and scientists.

We have been collecting, writing and discussing the activities in this book since 1991 and are excited to offer them *now* to teachers. We have included the activities which we tend to teach the most. Chapters are organized largely by mathematical concepts, and somewhat by dance categories. Chapters 1–3 involve counting in some fashion, chapter 4 is spatial in focus and serves as a segue into the rest of the chapters, which address geometry in a variety of ways. Chapters 9 through 12 involve an easily constructed prop. We hope this organization for the book will help teachers choose the appropriate exercise to fit the mathematics they are working on.

We are not proposing that these activities replace traditional math or traditional dance instruction — though that is a provocative idea for the future! This book is designed for those crucial junctures when a concept needs to be understood mentally, physically and emotionally. Or for the infusion of energy and excitement that classes sometimes need. Or to reach those students whose learning styles are not compatible with traditional methods of teaching. Or for teachers and students who want to experience dance and mathematics in a new way.

Once the concepts we have introduced are felt and thought, educators can return to the subjects with renewed vigor, and study individual areas in more depth.

Why Math and Dance?

At first glance it might seem that mathematics, that realm of rationality, and dance, that art of physical and emotional expression, have little in common. In our own experience as dancers and mathematicians, however, the two subjects are inextricably linked. When we choreograph a new dance or investigate a mathematical problem we are doing much the same thing: creatively exploring patterns in space and time with an eye toward aesthetic potential.

As we have shared our perspective in teacher workshops, we have witnessed spontaneous and inadvertent acts that confirm our belief that, rather than being separate educational areas, the physical and the mental belong together. After a performance of our basketball dance at a school in Santa Cruz County, for instance, a boy who looked to be in first or second grade ran after us and said, "You know, I was just playing basketball and I realized that I was dancing!"

Sometimes the students, or we ourselves, have been surprised by what happens. At an elementary school in Hawai'i, when we announced to a group of fifth graders that we were going to do math and dance, students in the class pointed to one girl and said, "She's good at math!" As the workshop progressed, other students excelled. One boy was extremely adept at the rhythmic exercises. Another girl was adept with rotational symmetry. The class was very surprised and began to see that there are many examples of mathematical thinking.

Sometimes schools have taken our work farther than we anticipated. At the Alabama High School of Fine Arts in Birmingham, a group of seniors created a performance with giant tangrams (chapters 11 & 12) which they used to recruit new students into the school. They then taught the performance to a group from the next year's graduating class.

Though the sentiment has been expressed in many ways, one school in northern Nevada stands out. A teacher said, "I wish my desire to move had been used as a tool to learn math when I was a kid."

Our work in educational settings, from the most elaborately funded private schools to some of the least supported public schools, has demonstrated that teachers who are willing to engage students with alternative methods are often quite successful. These methods allow for a variety of learning styles and cultural backgrounds, and also keep that spark of curiosity alive.

To us, the question is not "Why combine mathematics and dance, the creative and the cognitive, in class?" but rather "Why were they ever separated in the first place?"

Creating our First Show

In 1989, after having collaborated for three years on dances, two of us (Karl Schaffer and Erik Stern) began talking about the similarities between dance and mathematics.

Our discussions covered a wide range of topics. We noticed that math and dance both deal with codified concepts, such as symmetry, spatial awareness, counting problems and patterns. We also noticed aesthetic similarities: the need for internal consistency, the goal of striking a balance between analysis and intuition, and how either one could be abstract as well as worldly.

You could even sweat doing both, we realized.

These nascent ideas led us to create a performance designed for students, educators and families. As we worked on the show, we became convinced of its value; we also began to see how difficult it was going to be to make our vision clear and accessible. As teachers or professionals who cross established boundaries know, building a bridge between disciplines that is easily traversed is a daunting task.

We contacted the California Math Council-North and inquired if our performance might be appropriate for their next conference. Sherry Fraser, then program chair, said, "Well, can I see it?" She drove to Santa Cruz to watch the work in progress. After discussing our approach with us, she booked us as the opening event for the 1990 conference at Asilomar. Sherry's intelligence and enthusiasm gave us encouragement and feedback we needed.

At that time mathematics educators and organizations were re-evaluating not only how mathematics was taught, but how it was viewed. Rapid development of information technology fueled change in mathematics as well. Calculators that freed students from the constant drudgery of manual computation led to new demands that mathematics be exploratory and involve higher level thinking. Efforts to develop artificial intelligence came side-by-side with new understandings of how human intelligence and learning really work, leading to demands for multiple approaches in teaching math. And mathematics was changing itself as new areas such as chaos theory and fractals joined the discrete math topics more relevant to a world of computers.

Besides being professional dancers, we had the backgrounds which allowed us to look into the science side of things: Karl Schaffer was and is a mathematics professor and Erik Stern's undergraduate degree is in biology. Our own experiences in education had led us to see that other approaches in the sciences could be valuable. The then recently published National Council of Teachers of Mathematics (NCTM) Standards confirmed our feelings that concepts such as estimation and number sense, symmetry and spatial thinking, were as relevant to math education as the operations of arithmetic.

We also drew on the numerous performances we had seen and participated in that sought to link the arts with the curriculum. However, when it came to dance and science, we felt that little had been done, and what had been done skimmed the surface. The performances we saw were either more committed to the art or more committed to the science, but did not seem to have a firm foundation in both. When we did find efforts to use movement with mathematics they were usually centered on the pre-kindergarten and primary grades. Our extension of movement/mathematics activities to secondary and college levels has remained a hallmark of our work.

We were inspired to try out our own ideas by the numerous choreographers, composers, visual artists and playwrights who have addressed mathematics, either by imbedding the ideas of mathematics into the art itself, or by treating the subject more topically. The more we delved into math dance, the more we encountered performers, mathematicians and enthusiasts who were also exploring these links.

As with these other artists, our hopes for the project extended beyond an interest in sharing with audiences mathematical concepts. The project was a great opportunity to do for dance what mathematics education reformers wanted to do for math; that is, to make dance accessible, show its presence in everything we do, and expand the ways it is typically taught.

To us, dance and mathematics were more than equals, they were manifestations of the same interest in aesthetics and form, thought and expression. Presenting them in this light, we hoped, would also convey that the vast divide between the arts and sciences, one which includes funding and value differences, was a divide borne of misconceptions. The perception of dance and mathematics (and, by implication, art and science) as incompatible did not reflect the nature of these two essential endeavors — at least as we experienced them.

We knew, as all people involved in the arts know, that mathematics will always be required, but the arts are ever on precarious ground. The arts in America are too often left to the individual teacher, principal, school or district and are rarely given the imprimatur of national attention and funding. Mathematics would always be taught; dance would not. We wanted to share our beliefs in the strength and compatibility of these subjects.

Interestingly enough, dance had gone through a similar historical process as math education. The innovations of the 60's and 70's sought dance in the everyday, and also led to the question "What is dance?" But the results of these rarefied investigations did not trickle down to public schools.

Our first step in creating the performance was to look at the dances we had already made or were in the process of making, in terms of their appeal from both a choreographic and mathematical point of view.

The first dance we looked at was called "Private Fly," in which two guys in trench coats dance with fly swatters. In addition to types of symmetries we normally think of, such as reflection and rotation, the fly swatters got progressively larger, which introduced the symmetry of scale. The idea of symmetry is an underpinning of dance, though we later found that the different types of symmetry are rarely discussed in as explicit manner in choreographic classes as in mathematics classes.

Moreover, symmetry was also being reintroduced in math education by way of geometry. Fortunately for spatially and kinesthetically oriented students, this re-introduction of symmetry had students making, touching, drawing and visualizing geometric objects.

Other dances included in this first concert relating dance and mathematics:
- A tap dance, which dealt with patterns and some of the arithmetic associated with those patterns, and led to an audience interaction with interwoven rhythms.
- An almost vaudevillian hand-shake routine, which served to introduce the characters, and led to a discussion of estimation and number sense, as well as a workshop on counting handshakes.
- "Rotation," a trio for two dancers and a basketball, which led to a section in the performance about the physics of motion.

Our choreography and movement material showed that dance can arise from everyday activities (playing basketball, shaking hands, and even swatting flies). That we were taking stereotypical guy activities like sports and showing that they could be dance, broke the frequent stereotypes about dance. During *Two Guys Dancing About Math* we also tell the story of the mathematical work of Ada Lovelace, a 19th century mathematician who surmounted the barriers she faced.

It is hardly a secret that many people, including teachers, do not have a positive reaction to math class. The particular reasons may vary: a traumatic experience with math in the past, an unsupportive teacher, the symbols seem confusing, no allowance to work out problems in a way that is comfortable, acceptance of popular myths about who can succeed at math, or even a lack of aptitude (though this last one seems more rare).

The upshot is the same: students who need to learn mathematics are not coming away with the skills and knowledge required of them. Of equal importance, or maybe the root cause of the problem, is that students weak in math are not confident and enthused about the subject.

We were acutely aware of these responses to mathematics and interested in incorporating them into our performance. As a result, two rather opposite characters surfaced: one was analytic, Dr. Schaffer; the other, instinctive, Mr. Stern.

We wanted to show that there are many ways to do and experience mathematics and dance. We wanted students and teachers to get a sense of the different ways people can learn and express their love of various subjects.

When we premiered *Dr. Schaffer and Mr. Stern: Two Guys Dancing About Math* at the 1990 Asilomar Conference, the idea that our fascination would be of the same interest to others seemed a little unlikely. But, as it turns out, it has crossed the 400 performances and ten-year mark and is still in demand.

When we showed up at schools, kids, and sometimes even teachers, said things like "What are you gonna do, multiply with your bodies?" Our reply was usually "Just wait and see the show."

Afterwards, these questions made us want to clarify for ourselves the conceptual basis of what we were doing. In our show, dance was not a kind of mnemonic device. It was not the dance version of "Thirty days hath September, April, June and November…" Nor were we only using the body as a way of understanding concepts, and then discarding the expression inherent in the act of moving. The use of manipulatives has long been a part of education, and recently has experienced a much needed revival; however, the body, to us, is more than a big "manipulative." Its use can be an end in itself; moreover, the attention to aesthetics and perceptions that dance leads to is of equal value to the introduction of concepts.

We were looking to exploit the most basic ideas that underlie dance and mathematics, and, though those underlying ideas may seem absurdly simple, we felt they could lead to very clear and interesting problems both in the realm of art and science.

At its most complex and abstract, mathematics appears to be very far from dance or anything physical and palpable. Its concepts and symbols are manipulated by rules that sometimes appear mysterious; its purpose seems to be for the enjoyment or productiveness of those who practice it (and for the pain of many others).

But what is mathematics at its most basic level? Quantity, size, relationship, shape and space, reasoning, discerning patterns, representing a concept by a word or a symbol. And even before these ideas come abilities which could be called "pre-mathematical" thinking skills.

Included in the pre-mathematical category of concepts are bigger and smaller, same and different, before and after, including and excluding, inside and outside; and also remembering where you are and where you are going. We believe that the understanding of mathematics begins in the physical realm with these concepts.

To our way of thinking, this list of pre-mathematical skills is very close to pre-dancical (to coin a word) skills. A young dancer also needs to know before and after, same and different, and so on. These essential skills are the predecessors to dance and mathematics, and constitute the essential overlap of the disciplines.

From the Stage to the Classroom

Schools continued requesting that we get children and teachers doing what we were doing on stage; moving and thinking, thinking and moving. The first workshops we offered were extensions of the ideas explored in our concert, adapted to be safe and accessible. Later, after collaborating with Scott Kim on performances and workshops, our creative process sometimes went the other way: a workshop idea might lead to a new dance.

In all cases, the exercises were designed to be dualistic in the best sense. Ideally, students and teachers should be able to slip naturally from the exercises into significant mathematical explorations; they also should be able to take the exercises and choreograph studies which they could then perform for each other, the rest of the school, the P.T.A., or even the public.

Math Dance

Our work in the classroom has shown us that the ideas in mathematics are interesting to most everyone. The methods by which math is taught, however, can be a barrier. The interactive, visible, communicative properties of dance/movement can help bring mathematics to a comprehensible level.

Similarly, our work has shown us that the pure human energy of dance is universally interesting; the impulse is in everyone. But when the dancing is abstruse, people worry; when they feel they have to know the language of dance, that can also present a barrier.

Whole-body, expressive, mathematical activities introduce new elements into the classroom that go beyond traditional manipulatives. Here is a list of some of the attributes of what we like to call *math dance*:

Everyone participates. For example, one chapter has a trio of students create and explore three-fold rotationally symmetric shapes with their entire bodies. The exercise demands that everyone experience and demonstrate the mathematical concepts being introduced.

A deeper spatial thinking challenge. With manipulatives we can see what we are creating. With the entire body, we seem to operate from a three-dimensional picture in our minds. We suspect that using the entire body requires different (and at times more difficult) spatial thinking skills.

Kinesthetic learners. Individuals who learn kinesthetically find an experiential base to help them understand. Those who are less kinesthetically inclined get experiences that are often missing the higher one goes in the educational system.

Engages students. Involving one's body is exciting and memorable. It excites student interest.

New approach. The size of the product and the contrast between kinesthetic and, for example, symbolic mathematics, pushes students and teachers towards new insights and questions.

Communication. The scale of the exploration is expressive, and therefore allows students to experience mathematics as art and communication, and vice versa. In many cultures, arithmetic, spatial thinking and other mathematical skills are taught through stories, songs, games, and dances. The idea of mathematics as communication stimulates an interest in math that is broader, and forces students to develop their mathematical (as well as artistic) communication skills.

Aesthetics. Art deals with aesthetics; mathematicians feel that math is intrinsically beautiful and has other aesthetic qualities as well. Observing, responding to what is observed, and articulating that response (sometimes labeled "aesthetic valuing"), are skills that must be developed. "What seems better and why?" is a question which is an integral part of creating dances, a question which is posed, in various forms, throughout this book.

Helps students cross barriers. Introduces students to new areas; those who are unfamiliar with dance are given a route into this performing art. Those who are shy of math are similarly helped to find a way to experience it. For example, a unit which involves the manipulation of giant tangrams, where each person carries only one of the seven shapes, provides an excellent way to explore geometric principles and also can lead to story-telling, art, and dance.

Social event. The group and kinesthetic aspect of this work makes it public, and involves students in social interactions. Discussion and group work grow naturally out of the explorations. Dance becomes a less solitary venture, and mathematics becomes a clear intellectual, physical and social event to which teachers can refer.

Culture. The burgeoning field of ethnomathematics has drawn attention to how much mathematical thinking is present in all aspects of culture. Dance and mathematical thinking are found in all cultures, and we have tried to point to particular forms of dance that deal with mathematical ideas in interesting ways. This kind of work can lead to new respect for diverse cultures, and help integrate learning about culture into the classroom.

Expands each discipline. As we began to find our way teaching workshops, we noticed that movement was encouraging experimentation. It was pushing people away from inflexibility and toward play and interaction, away from a rigid search for right answers that is often associated with mathematics and toward the sort of play and interaction that mathematicians experience. Similarly the work shows the connection dance has to ideas and forms of analysis that are not always associated with the discipline.

For specific directions on how to use this book and helpful preparatory information, please read the next chapter *How To Use This Book*.

How to Use this Book

Choose a topic. This book is for classroom teachers who want to introduce ideas in mathematics and dance in a vivid, memorable way. The activities are intended to supplement the conventional curriculum. Feel free to skip directly to chapters that relate to material you want to teach in class. The topics are described in the table of contents. The only chapters that need to be done in sequence are the three symmetry chapters 5-7 (*Threesies*, *Watch Your p's and q's*, and *Twisted Addition*), and the two tangram chapters 11 and 12 (*Moving with Giant Tangrams* and *Storytelling with Giant Tangrams*).

Set up your space. Most of the activities in this book require space for students to stand up and move around. We recommend you push desks to the edge of the classroom, or move to a large open space like a gym or multipurpose room. Students should be dressed comfortably: loose-fitting rather than tight clothes, physical education attire is not necessary. As with any physical activity safety is a concern. Remove sharp objects, and make sure students have room to move safely.

Prepare materials. Most chapters require no materials, except for pencil and paper. The last four chapters require simple props which you will need to make: loops of string, poles tied together, and giant tangrams. Instructions for making props are at the ends of chapters.

Do the activities. Every chapter includes a series of activities, starting simply and getting more involved. Start at the beginning and stop when you run out of time or reach material that is too challenging for the students.

Discuss and reflect. After doing the activities, have students reflect on their experiences by discussing questions and concepts in the Reflections and Assessment section at the end of each chapter. You will also find assessment guidelines and further activities here, as well as book, video and web resources.

Who Is this Book For?

For everyone. You do not have to be a trained dancer or mathematician to use this book, and neither do your students. That is because our activities address the most basic, universal elements of dance and mathematics — walking, counting, moving, making shapes — that are equally accessible to beginners and experts. On the other hand if you do have expertise in dance or mathematics you will find more advanced material at the ends of chapters that will challenge you to go further. In most cases we have written as if the reader is a teacher, even though we hope that others interested in what we are doing — students, parents, mathematicians, dancers — will also read and try the activities.

For students of all ages. One of the strengths of the arts is that it spans ages and cultures. A five-year-old child and a graduate student can listen to the same piece of music by Ellington or Stravinsky, and each get something out of the experience. Artists are constantly returning to the basics — musicians return to rhythm and melody, visual artists return to line and shape, dancers return to balance and movement. Mathematicians too find value in re-evaluating the most basic ideas — mathematician John Conway recently rethought the concept of a number and came up with a new way of analyzing games.

The essential ideas that begin each chapter are applicable to any level. The level of the student, of course, dictates the extent to which each exercise is taken. For example, Chapter 3, *Heads or Tails* deals with probability. Everyone can do the first exercise, which asks students to flip a coin and to remember a few movements of the participants' own making, so the movement difficulty is variable. On the other hand, each chapter poses challenges towards the end. Chapter 3 concludes with a look at the complexities of tossing multiple coins and also asks students to consider dances that have pushed the boundaries of art by incorporating randomness.

Tips for younger students. Younger students may do some tasks better in smaller groups, and may prefer to perform for each other within their groups rather than for the whole class. They may be less inhibited than teenagers or adults, and actually have less trouble with some exercises. Because their motor skills are less developed, safety issues are more important. Although it is best to stick with simpler exercises, sometimes it is important to challenge students with material that they are not quite ready for, without demanding that they succeed right away.

Tips for older students. Older students may be able to move through more of the exercises faster, but should still work through the opening warm-up exercises. The warm-ups introduce the ideas of the chapter and allow the teacher to assess the students' readiness for the main activities. Self-consciousness about their appearance doing movement may be more of an issue for older students; we have tried to deal with this by using everyday movement rather than dance class movement, and to introduce them to the idea of performing for their peers. See the more advanced exercises in the *Further Activities* section of each chapter. Look for *Math Tips* and *Dance Tips* throughout the chapters that explore interesting issues in more depth. Sometimes older students should be assigned to investigate these either in small groups or as individual research projects, and report back to the class.

Our Approach to Dance

Here are the most important things to know about our approach to dance, especially if you have not taught dance — or even taken a dance class — before.

Ordinary movement. Our work is based on the proposition that both mathematics and dance are present in everyday events and tasks. Therefore, students need not imitate trained dancers. Ballet and hip-hop moves are welcome additions, but not required. Instead we ask students to create their own movements, based on their individual abilities, knowledge, and desires. Everyday movement is fine. We have seen students bring tumbling or soccer movements into this work. Special Education classes have worked with these same exercises in ways that accommodated their limitations.

We want our work to welcome non-dancers to dance. Students work in small groups before performing for larger groups. Several of the activities use a limited range of motion: the hands or feet. Several activities use props, which tends to make students less self-conscious, since the audience's focus goes first to the props rather than the bodies of the performers. We try to engage the creativity of the students from the get-go, so they can participate more fully in the art form.

Done fully. Although we do not place expectations on what movements students use, we do want them to move with clarity and conviction. So long as students commit to their choices, most choices are acceptable. Your role as teacher is to get students to push their limits, engage their whole bodies, and explore ideas fully. Sometimes students feel tentative, and the uncertainty shows in their movement. Discerning the difference between calm and tentative can be tricky. We trust you to know when to push and when to ease back. If nothing else, watching students dance will tell you more about them. The body, like the eyes, is a mirror to the soul.

For an audience. For us dance is a performing art, and its goal is artistic expression on stage before an audience. This is not to deny the importance of, for example, the sense of community found in folk dance, the physical benefits of aerobic dance, or even the ceremonial aspects of liturgical dance, all of which are usually not performed on stage. When you do dance for an audience, certain basic problems arise. You immediately run into the problem that you cannot see what you are doing. You have to imagine how your movements look from the outside. So it becomes important to ask other people to review your work, and to develop your own eye for looking at dance. Mirrors and video can also help you see yourself move. The cognitive skill of moving and knowing how your movement looks can take a lifetime to develop.

It's noisy. A dance class sounds and feels very different from a traditional mathematics class. It is not reasonable to assume students will do this work quietly. We find that when we lead educators through these exercises, they are as loud as third graders (if not more)! Allowing periods of unruly energy is okay, as long as students are encouraged to focus afterwards. Set reasonable guidelines and reinforce them. The perennial friend of dance teachers is the word "freeze!" If a teacher can make stillness or quietness a release of energy and something on which to focus, it can work to that teacher's advantage.

Once in San Francisco we had a class that seemed to be split down the middle between the rowdy and the reflective. We taught them the Hand Shake exercises (Chapter 1, *How Many Ways To Shake Hands?*), which led to shockingly divergent results: we saw groups running and jumping at each other, connecting hands in mid-air or in a lunged position upon landing. We saw ordered, intricate intertwinings of arms and hands, while the rest of the body stayed calm. Both approaches are fine. Expect to see both.

It takes space. When you move your whole body, you need room to move. Although a few of our activities can be done sitting down, most require a large open space. You can push desks to the sides of the room, or find an empty space like a gym or multipurpose room. You can also work outside, but concrete and grass surfaces can be difficult to work on, you will have to shout to be heard, and there may be many distractions.

Modern dance. Our work is in the tradition of "modern dance," which seeks to explore diverse ways of looking at and manipulating movement. Modern dance embraces all sorts of movement, not just one style. In our own performances, for instance, we have drawn from tap, Flamenco, martial arts, sports, and ballet, as well as from everyday movement. Modern dancers often refer to the dance studio as a laboratory in which dancers and choreographers experiment, and describe movement in terms of three elements taken from the vocabulary of physics: **space**, **time**, and **energy**. Of course dance is not just physics: remember that it may serve the needs of ceremony, community, exercise, psychology, storytelling, competition, politics, personal growth, artistic expression, or professional aspirations. Be open to whatever form of expression students bring to their work.

However, these elements of space, time, and energy may be helpful to remember when you look at the movements that students do. If students seem stuck or want direction, paying attention to these aspects of movement can help you find suggestions for improvement or further development.

Following is a list of sub-categories and descriptive words of these three dance elements. The list is presented to jump start non-dancers' thinking about the art of dance; it is not complete, as any dancer or choreographer will tell you. There are many excellent books about dance and the creative process, and we encourage teachers to read further, or, better still, go see many different types of dance. In the descriptions below, aspects of dance are depicted individually, but when one is dancing, one is engaged in many or all of these aspects at once. After all, we all occupy space, are present in time, and have a certain quality or energy at any given moment.

Space. The parts of the body can be used to create shapes. The shapes may have different **levels**, usually divided into low, medium, and high The levels are relative, though medium usually refers to the height of the body as we walk normally. The body can also move through space. These motions create **directions**, **paths**, and **floor patterns** All of these aspects of space involve dimension: the movements may occur in a line, along a flat plane, or curve through space. They are enhanced or affected by the performer's **focus**, which indicates not only where the dancer's attention is, but also how the effort of the movement is concentrated.

Time. All movement takes place in time, and has **duration**. Repetition of movement can create **rhythms**. The most essential repetition which underlies a rhythm is its **pulse** or **beat** The speed of a beat determines the **tempo**. To stress a beat creates an **accent**. A single rhythmic pattern can be composed of many of these aspects of time.

Energy. Energy refers to the quality with which a movement is performed – the how of the movement. Energy can be looked at in a variety of ways: the emotional (e.g. angry, ecstatic, pensive, afraid), the muscular (e.g. bound, flowing, contractive, relaxed), the initiation (e.g. from the center, peripherally - from the ends of the limbs, or starting at the top of the body and moving down). Examples of words used frequently to describe qualities of motion include swing, suspend, percussive, sustained, collapse, extend, contract, and rebound.

Other elements of dance. In addition to the dance elements there are descriptions and analyses of how the body operates. These descriptions take different forms, such as the parts of the body (e.g. head, torso, arms, legs, hips), the motions of the joints (e.g. flexion, extension, adduction, abduction), and what are called basic locomotor patterns (walk, run, hop, jump, leap, skip, gallop, and slide).

The study of dance will greatly help anyone interested in applying the exercises in this book; however it bears repeating that this is not a requirement. People use and understand movement naturally, and this serves as an excellent basis for our work. Pay attention to how one feels when doing a movement, the mechanics of how it is achieved, and how it looks. Interest in and commitment to movement can go a long way towards teaching oneself about the art of movement.

Lastly, a word about safety. In our experience, children and adults pose different safety concerns. Children are more likely to hurt themselves or others due to carelessness, not because their muscles are not ready to move. They may collide with objects or each other when getting carried away or when going a bit wild. Make certain the room is as free of dangerous objects as possible. If the students remove their shoes, have them remove their socks as well, to prevent them from slipping. When introducing movement assignments have students begin slowly. Keep an eye out for potential hazards or students who seem to lack self-control. Students who lack self-control often love to move, as it helps them become familiar with their bodies, learn what the results of physical actions are, and simply release energy. Nevertheless, these students can benefit from, and sometimes require, individual attention.

Particularly if they are not accustomed to moving, adults' muscles and joints might not be as ready for activity as children's. Start slowly with adults as well, to allow muscles and joints to warm up, and also to allow them to take stock of their bodies and what they are able to do. Children are often ready, willing and able to do explosive movements after just a few minutes of class. Adults are not. Unless certain of the adults' capabilities, do not encourage them too much in this direction: let them choose the nature and intensity of their movements.

Our Approach to Mathematics

Here are the most important things to know about our approach to mathematics, especially if you have not taught mathematics before.

Beyond arithmetic. There is more to mathematics than arithmetic or the procedures of algebra. The mathematical topics in this book also include geometry and symmetry, probability, and combinatorics (the mathematics of counting combinations), among others. Furthermore we are interested in developing the perceptual and cognitive skills that underlie mathematical thinking, such as visualizing shapes, discerning quantity, defining problems, recognizing patterns, and thinking systematically.

Experience followed by reflection. Our approach to teaching mathematics will be familiar to those comfortable with the educational philosophy behind manipulatives: give students physical experiences to explore in a directed but open-ended way, then ask students to reflect on their experiences by recording, analyzing, and discussing them. Only after students have explored the ideas physically do we ask them to work with abstract symbolic notation. All too often students are introduced to abstract ideas without a bridge to concrete experience, and their understanding shatters if the problems they are given are not exactly the same as in the book. When students make connections between physical experience and abstract thinking, their understanding is more resilient and can stretch to fit new situations. Recent research indicates that movement activity is not subsidiary to thinking, but is as central to human beings as intellect and emotion.

Right answers later. Early in our work, we tried to push the concepts, the "right answers," too soon. In other words, before students had experienced the exercises, we were asking them to conceptualize and know the material. Our performances and workshops have taught us to let students voice their thoughts and opinions without editing. For instance, in Chapter 1, *How Many Ways to Shake Hands?*, we found that students came up with many different answers to a problem we gave them. Rather than tell them immediately the one answer we thought was right, we learned to let students defend their various answers based on their interpretations of the problem. The discussion helped students clarify their understanding of the problem, and even taught us some new solutions that we had not considered.

Math as a creative art. Mathematics is often taught as a series of rote procedures to memorize, just as dance is often taught as a series of rote moves to perfect. Even progressive mathematics textbooks rarely assume that students will make new mathematical discoveries. There is another side to mathematics: the creative process that mathematicians go through when they create (or discover) new mathematics. Four steps are often present in this process: asking questions about a situation, investigating answers for particular cases, noticing patterns, and generalizing the results. Sometimes the creation of new mathematics, like other artistic work, is unplanned and seems to follow no pre-set pattern. Mathematicians often speak of the role of intuition and imagination in their work. In this book we are trying to build imaginative connections to and within mathematical thinking.

Combining Math and Dance

Here are the most important things to know about our approach to combining mathematics and dance. For more about our philosophy and the history of our work, see the *Introduction*.

Both are creative pursuits. In our work as dancers, mathematicians and teachers, we have been interested in the area of overlap in which mathematics and dance address a similar goal: the creative exploration of formal patterns. In dance this is closer to what choreographers do when they create new dances than to what performers do when they practice particular moves. In mathematics this is closer to what mathematicians do when they create new mathematics than to what engineers do when they apply particular formulas to get practical results. The activities in this book concern creative process, not technique. However, the creative processes serve as excellent stepping stones to understanding mathematical technique, if you will, and dance technique.

Both pulls are important. We have seen interesting efforts to combine mathematics and dance in which one illustrates the other. For instance, a mathematician might have people join hands in complicated patterns to illustrate a concept in topology. Or a choreographer might mix repetitious and random movements by the dancers to convey the notions of chaos theory. This is fine, and you will find many similar exercises in this book. But we are just as interested in developing the same exercises in an imaginative direction. For instance, we might also ask students to develop a dance based on a pattern of joining hands, or play with, rather than try to depict, ideas about order and disorder. Throughout this book you will find that the exercises pull alternately in the directions of physical dance performance and mathematical exploration.

Each enriches the others. We expect that many teachers will use this book to teach either mathematics or dance specifically. However, we encourage you to keep the two subjects integrated, and push students in both physical and intellectual directions simultaneously. Mathematics and dance can enrich each other. Don't leave your mind behind when you dance, and don't leave your body behind when you do math.

Kinesthetic learning. Our work with math dance is part of a larger movement to reintroduce sensory and kinesthetic experiences in education, and support them with involvement in the arts. Some educational traditions, such as Montessori and Waldorf, have always made the arts and kinesthetic experience central to the learning environment. The focus on manipulatives in current elementary classrooms is based on the belief that visual, tactile, and kinesthetic experience is important to learning. Bodily-kinesthetic intelligence is one of the seven basic intelligences proposed by influential psychologist Howard Gardner. We sometimes find that students who are natural kinesthetic learners (they may be the students with a lot of energy who cannot seem to sit still) blossom when taught kinesthetically, while students who prefer other modes of thinking are challenged by kinesthetic activities, even if the concepts are familiar.

Adding Music

Throughout the book we suggest teachers put on music to accompany students' demonstrations of the exercises. Usually it is at the end of a section where students have been putting together movements into longer sequences that we suggest playing music. Music works many wonders: it organizes students by giving them an aural environment in which to dance; the tempo can encourage students to work together; when music is playing there is less tendency to talk; music turns a demonstration into a performance; and, last but not least, it makes people want to dance their movements rather than just go through the motions.

Though we encourage you to use music that you feel suits the dance itself or the mood of the class that day, here are a few suggestions based on our experiences.

Categories. Music can be divided into many different categories. Here are three categories that we have found helpful. We suggest that if you have three different examples from each of the following categories, you will be prepared for anything the students make up: 1) three tempos, fast, medium and slow; 2) three different instrumentations, such as orchestral, electronic and folk instruments; 3) three different qualities of music. This last category can be taken many different ways. Examples of qualities are upbeat or down, hopeful or dark, light or heavy, frenetic or calm.

Energy level. When selecting a piece of music to accompany student demonstrations, ask yourself, "What is the overall energy level of the dances the students are performing? What would I like the energy level to be?" Putting on music which is too loud or energetic can drown out the movement, in the same way bright clothing can obscure a nice tie or piece of jewelry. Also, ask yourself what the overall quality is. Quirky? Regal? Patient? Smooth? How can music enhance that quality? Sometimes contrast can help reveal movement, as with serene music accompanying dances with occasional explosions of energy.

Wordless. Avoid songs with lyrics. Lyrics can complicate a performance needlessly. The students have enough to deal with in terms of the mathematics and the movement; lyrics tend to add a third intrusive element which can seem to comment on the dance. Sometimes lyrics lead performers to act out the words. Though there is nothing wrong with this in and of itself, the activities in this book are designed to get students to express themselves with their bodies. Language, unless it is an integral part of the dance, can distract from that physical expression.

Avoid strong associations. Avoid music which carries with it strong associations. For example, playing the theme to Star Wars can contribute energy, but also could get students more interested in imitating their favorite characters than putting their focus into doing and feeling the movements they have been working on.

All styles. There are so many types of music that creating a list is not only impossible, it invariably skips important music. With that in mind, here is a short, off-the-top-of-the-head list of composers whose work often fulfills the criteria above: **J.S. Bach, Tito Puente, Mickey Hart, Duke Ellington, Igor Stravinsky, Mozart, Hildegard von Bingen, Scott Joplin** and **Brian Eno**. Styles of music include folk, ethnic, techno, classical, baroque, jazz, blue-grass, motets, ambient and funk.

Encourage listening. Putting on music to accompany dance is a great way to introduce new types of music to students. People often resist listening to music which is new to them, for the simple reasons that unfamiliar sounds or arrangements of sounds can be jarring. However, one listens different when one is about to perform, because of the investment in the outcome. For many people, moving to music is a fuller experience than passively listening. Moving encourages listening not only with the ears, but also with the body, making one more open to new sounds.

Have fun. Having said all this, just have fun with your choices. After all, you can always change to a different piece of music the next time around.

CHAPTER 1
How Many Ways to Shake Hands?
A new look at an everyday gesture

Grades:	K–12
Time:	25-45 minutes
Math Concepts:	Counting, combinations, problem definition
Dance Concepts:	Sequence, dynamics
Groups of:	2, 3
Space:	Regular classroom with desks moved to sides, or larger
Materials:	none
Prerequisites:	none
Related activities:	Chapter 5 *Threesies* and Chapter 8 *Hand Figures* also use hands.

We all shake hands. Some handshakes are ordinary, some are more unusual. Kids are especially creative with handshakes, often inventing complex "secret" handshakes.

In this activity we approach handshakes with some fresh questions. What are some new ways to shake hands? How many ways can two people shake hands? How can all pairs of people in a group shake hands? These questions lead us deep into specific mathematical problems as well as open-ended movement exercises.

When we first taught these exercises, we hoped to get the "right" answers to the basic mathematical questions we posed. The more we taught the exercise, the more we learned that students would come up with unexpected answers no matter how clearly the rules were stated (or we thought they were stated). The students' alternate answers were based on differing interpretations of the parameters we set. We grew to value the discussions and disagreements about interpretations as much or more than the "right" answer. After all, much of mathematics and science involves making decisions about what is counted and what is not.

The inspiration for using handshakes as a way into math and dance in the classroom came from the opening dance in *Dr. Schaffer and Mr. Stern: Two Guys Dancing About Math*. In this almost vaudevillian handshake sequence, the two characters cannot seem to shake hands, and then when they succeed, they find they are stuck! When we first started doing math dance workshops for teachers, we looked at our dances anew, and found that the variety of handshakes in our opening sequence made us wonder how many ways there are to shake hands.

1–1. Secret Handshakes (3-5 minutes)

This quick warm up activity gets students thinking about handshakes creatively. Have students work in pairs. If there is an odd number of students, a trio will also work.
- "What's the biggest handshake you can make up? What's the smallest?"
- "What's the most unusual handshake you can make up? Try do something different from what anyone else is doing."
- "Make up a handshake for creature from another planet that expresses something about their culture."
- "What 'secret' handshakes do you already know? Can you start with those and change them somehow?"
- Use any or all of the questions that follow which are designed to help students focus on manipulating particular aspects of their handshakes: "Can you pull away from the handshake in a different way than you got into the handshake? How low can you do the handshake? How high? Can the handshake have two or three or more parts to it? Can you use fingers, wrists, elbows or even legs in the handshake? Can there be parts that are faster or slower? Can you reach under, over or around each other in the handshake?"

1–2. Counting Handshakes (5 minutes)

In this mathematical activity students count how many ways hands can be combined.
- Normally people shake hands with their right hands. But you can also use your left hand. Have students work in pairs, and ask "How many ways are there for two people to shake hands, if each person uses either their left or right hand, but not both? All that matters is which hand each person uses: right hand to right hand counts as only one handshake, no matter how you do it."
- Ask students to record their answers on paper, including both the number of handshakes, and what each handshake is. Students can record their answers using words, pictures, or a combination of both.
- You may wish to ask each group to perform their handshakes in a sequence that includes each handshake just once. Have a few groups perform their handshake sequences for the rest of the class.

The answer we originally had in mind is four handshakes:

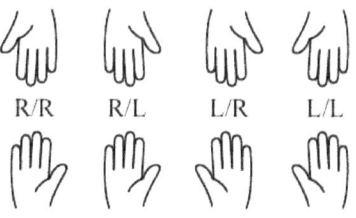

Four handshakes

However we have found that students often come up with other answers that are just as valid. Rather than insist that our answer is the only right answer, we prefer to have students explain their answers, whether or not they agree with ours. Answers we have heard range from "two" to "six" to "infinite" to "it depends." Here are two other answers based on different interpretations of what counts as a handshake:

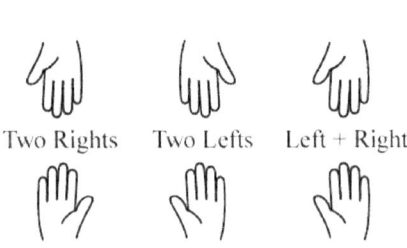

Two Rights   Two Lefts   Left + Right

Three handshakes

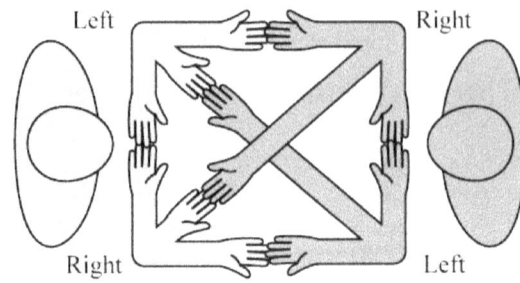

Six handshakes =
four shaking other person + two shaking self

- After the discussion, show the students our method of counting which is diagrammed above. They might not all agree with our method.
- It is valuable to let students defend their answers based on their interpretations of the rules. Discussing different interpretations of the rules will help the class come to a clearer understanding of just what the rules are. We are not saying all answers are correct; what matters is that students count handshakes in a manner consistent with their interpretation of the rules. In the examples above, for instance, the answer "four handshakes" is based on an interpretation that distinguishes who is shaking with which hand, whereas the answer "three handshakes" makes no such distinction.

1–3. Counting Double-Handed Handshakes (5-10 minutes)

This is a harder version of the Counting Handshakes exercise. Again, students must think carefully about how to count combinations of things.

- Have students get in groups of three. Ask each group to choose two people to be "Hand-shakers" and the other to be the "Counter."
- Ask the groups to figure out "How many ways are there for two people to shake hands, if each person can use either one or both hands at a time?" Remember, right to right counts as one handshake, no matter how you do it.
- Have groups demonstrate and count their handshakes. If time allows, have the class make a chart on the board similar to the chart we made above. Since students can use one or two hands, there are more choices.
- Again, the answers will undoubtedly vary from group to group. That is okay. The point is to have students explain their rules and demonstrate that their counts are consistent with those rules, not for everyone to get the same answer.
- Here is one answer: 4 ways to shake one hand to one hand + 4 ways to shake one hand to two hands + 2 ways to shake two hands to two hands = 10 handshakes. Note that this count does not include all four hands grasped together in a clump, a handshake that many students will include.

> **Math note: Problem solving strategies**
> In mathematics as well as in dance, it is important to give students open-ended activities in which they have room to develop their own strategies. Before you can count something abstract like handshakes, you must first figure out how to organize what you are counting so that you do not miss anything, and do not count anything twice. In everyday life we often encounter situations in which we need to improvise new ways to count things. This is not as easy as it sounds!

1–4. Handshake Dances (10-20 minutes)

In this movement exercise students develop a dance from a series of handshakes.
- Students are still in groups of three.
- For this activity, ask each group to make up a sequence of 3 to 6 handshakes. Use fewer handshakes for younger students. Any type of movement is acceptable, as long as it is safe.

If students want more direction, ask them these questions, or make up your own.
- "Can you make it really high, or really low? Can it involve a jump or a turn?"
- "How can you shake hands without using your hands?"
- "How can all three of you shake hands at the same time?"
- "What would it look like to shake hands under water?"
- "Can you think of a handshake that is completely different from any handshake you have seen before?"

Once each trio has decided on a handshake sequence, have them practice the sequence so they can do it clearly without hesitating and without talking. Urge students to think about the performance aspects of their handshake sequences.
- How do people meet? How do they separate? A strong beginning and end can add much to a dance.
- Try varying the dynamics, sometimes moving with exaggerated slowness, sometimes with great speed.
- Vary the mood. Make handshakes that are friendly, mysterious, mechanical, noble, sad, or nervous.

Once groups have mastered their sequences, you can challenge them to:
- Reverse the order of the handshakes in the sequence.
- Reverse the movements themselves (more difficult).
- Perform the mirror image: a right to left shake becomes a left to right shake.
- Construct transitions from one group's performance to another.

Have each group perform their sequence for the rest of the group.
- You may want to ask everyone who is not performing to sit down so people can see better.
- Decide on an order for the groups in the class (e.g. Tommy's group, then Jenny's group, etc.). Have the groups go in order and perform to music. Ask each group to be ready so they can start as soon as the previous group is finished.
- We find that adding music makes this activity feel more like a performance. See suggestions for music in *How to Use this Book* on page 15.

Dance note: Everyday movement

Everyday movements like shaking hands are a great way to involve non-dancers in doing and creating movement sequences. The gesture of shaking hands is familiar, so students do not feel intimidated. And creating new handshakes is fun, so students do not feel self-conscious. Yet as students practice and refine their handshake sequences, they quickly become engaged in the real challenges of choreography.

Although many types of dance, such as classical ballet, take years of practice to master, others are built on everyday movements that anyone can do. For instance the pop group N'Sync performs a dance sequence based on the act of sitting on a folding chair. The musical performance Stomp creates dance out of everyday actions like sweeping the floor. Many hip-hop moves began as everyday gestures. All over the world folk dances are made out of the everyday movements of work and play.

In the world of modern dance, the Judson Church movement in the 1960s gave rise to choreographers like Yvonne Rainer, Trisha Brown and Twyla Tharp, who used untrained dancers performing ordinary movements in their works. "Esplanade," by the Paul Taylor Dance Company, is built out of walking, running and jumping movements. Of course it takes concentration and focus to perform these dances well, but dances based on familiar movements are easier for audiences to relate to.

1–5. Reflection and Assessment

The Dance
To assess the dance, ask yourself:
- Did students remember their handshake sequences?
- Did they improve with practice?
- Did they commit to the movement?

Have students discuss the following questions:
- "How do people greet each other in other countries? How do you think the ritual of shaking hands started?"
- "Have you ever seen handshakes used in a dance? How were they used?"
- "What surprised you when you saw handshakes that other people invented?"
- "When you composed your own handshake dance, how did you handle the transitions from one handshake to another? What were some other ways you saw other groups handle transitions?"

After the groups of students have demonstrated their handshake dances or pair dances, have them practice so they can do their dances clearly and with energy. If one group of students comes up with a particularly fun sequence, have everyone learn it and perform it. Have students discuss the following:
- How did your dance change as you rehearsed and refined it?
- What was particularly challenging as you refined your dance?
- What sort of music would go with your dance?

Here are ways to take the handshake exercises further:
- What good ideas do you see in other people's dances that you could use in your own dances?
- What dance ideas came out of the handshake exercises that you could use for making other dances?
- When you are making other dances for other activities in this book, think back to the handshake exercise and steal good ideas from what you learned.
- Create a movement sequence that begins and ends with a handshake, but might do anything else in between.

The Mathematics
The counting handshakes exercise asks students to record their answers and defend their answers, based on how they defined "handshake." As students listen to the various answers, have them ask themselves:
- Is the explanation of what counts as a handshake clear and consistent with the assigned problem?
- For each answer for the number of possible handshakes, was the answer consistent with the interpretation of the rules? Were any combinations missed or counted twice?
- The statement of the counting handshakes problem is deliberately ambiguous, to allow for different interpretations of what counts as a handshake. "How could you restate the counting handshakes exercise to eliminate the ambiguity, so that only one of the answers that the class got would be correct? Can you change the problem statement to make another of the possible answers be the correct one?"

Recording your answers on paper helps you remember what you did, clarify your reasoning, and communicate your reasoning to other people.
- A week or month later, who can remember their secret handshakes? Reviewing the handshakes provides a good classroom fill-in activity.
- For the handshake counting activity, have students write descriptions, using both words and pictures, of what handshakes they counted. Do the diagrams clearly communicate what was counted and how? What are some of the different diagramming techniques that students used? Which techniques were most effective?
- Have students write descriptions of their handshake dances, using both words and pictures. Can another group reconstruct the sequence from the written description?

Ask advanced students to generalize the counting problems.
- How many handshakes are possible between two people if each person has three arms? Four arms? What is a formula that gives the answer for N arms? Can you prove that your formula is correct?
- Suppose people shook hands three people at a time, instead of two people at a time. How many different three-way handshakes are possible in a group of five people? Six people? Seven? What is a formula that gives the answer for the number of three-way handshakes in a group of N people? What about for the number of X-way handshakes in a group of Y people?
- What other counting questions can you ask about handshakes?

Math note: Combinatorics

The area of mathematics that deals with counting combinations of things is called combinatorics, which is part of discrete mathematics. The word "discrete" refers to discrete things like handshakes or people, which only occur in whole units, as opposed to continuous things, like water or speed, which occur in continually varying fractional quantities. Discrete mathematics has become more important in recent years because it is central in computer science. Combinatorics is one of the most accessible areas of modern mathematics, since many of the questions are easy for anyone to understand without much mathematical background.

1–6. Further Activities

Dances that connect hands. Many traditional dances involve connecting hands (Square Dances, Waltzes, Israeli and Greek Folk Dances). Why would this be? Is connecting hands a global tradition among peoples? Are there cultures that discourage connected hands? Are there cultures that have rules for connecting hands (either socially or in dances) that are different from ours? Why?

Here are other activities that involve acting out and counting systematic sequences of combinations.

Standing in line. In how many different orders can three people stand in a line? Can you make a movement sequence that includes every order just once? Try the same game with four or five people. Harder question: Can you find a way to move through each of the possible orders, without repeating any, by switching exactly two adjacent people at each step? This is easy for three people, difficult for four or more.

Holding hands. A group of four people stand in a circle. Everyone reaches into the center and grabs another person's hand with each hand. How many different ways are there for everyone in the group to hold one other person's hand in each hand? How many of these ways have everyone connected in one loop? How many have two loops? Make a movement sequence in which every person holds another hand in each hand without letting go.

Climbing stairs. How many different ways are there to walk up a flight of six stairs, if each time you take a step you can go up one or two steps? What about for a flight of seven stairs? Eight? What other rules can you make for going up a flight of stairs? Make a movement sequence based on going up and down stairs. Note: your answers will probably involve the Fibonacci sequence 1,1,2,3,5,8,13,21,34..., in which the first two numbers are both 1, and the next number in the sequence is always the sum of the previous two numbers.

Counting Pairs. A mathematical question leads to a movement sequence, which leads to an investigation in combinatorics.
- Have students work in groups of four. Larger groups are okay, but smaller groups are too small.
- Ask the groups to have each pair of people shake hands once. "How many handshakes are there altogether? How can you be sure you did not miss any handshakes or count a handshake twice? For this problem we do not care what the handshakes look like or which hands you use, we only care about who has shaken hands with whom."

- "Can you perform all the handshakes in sequence without repeating any? Can you find an order that is easy to remember?" Have groups rehearse their sequences and perform for the rest of the class.
- A harder question for group discussion: "If everyone in the class shook hands with everyone else just once, how many handshakes would there be?" The answer to this question is too big to figure out by trial and error. Instead, you need to develop a systematic way to find the number of pairs in a group of any size. Here is a hint. Figure out what the answer is for groups of 3, 4, 5, and 6 people. Then look for a pattern that lets you figure out the answers for 7, 8 and 9. Can you explain why the pattern works? Can you draw a picture that helps you count the pairs? By the way, this is just how mathematicians work: by asking a question, investigating small examples, then looking for patterns.

> **Dance note: Couples dances**
> Ballroom dances often use patterns that allow every boy to pair up with every girl. The simplest way to do this is for all the boys and all the girls to form two rings, one inside the other, then slowly parade one ring past the other. Square dancing uses more complex patterns that let couples exchange partners in all possible combinations.

1–7. Resources

Anno, Mitsumasa. *Anno's Mysterious Multiplying Jar*. Putnam, 1983. Engaging picture book that asks what 1 times 2 times 3 times…10 is? Reminiscent of the riddle about the man with seven wives with seven sacks with seven cats… Many of Anno's picture books for kids are excellent visualizations of mathematical ideas.

Banes, Sally. *Terpsichore in Sneakers: Post-Modern Dance*. Wesleyan Univ. Press, 1987. The philosophy and aesthetics of the postmodern dance movement in the United States, from 1960 to 1985.

Banes, Sally. *Democracy's Body: Judson Dance Theater, 1962-1964*. Duke Univ. Press (reprint), 1993. An historical account of Judson Dance Theater, the seminal postmodern dance community.

Kenney, Margaret J, ed. *Discrete Mathematics across the Curriculum, K-12: 1991 Yearbook*. Reston, VA: National Council of Teachers of Mathematics, 1991. Articles on discrete mathematics for the classroom. A good overview.

Nozaki, Akihiro, and Mitsumasa Anno. *Anno's Hat Tricks*. New York: Philomel Books, 1985. Logical puzzles with different arrangements of hats. Amusing and accessible to young kids, yet requires sophisticated reasoning.

Rosenstein, Joseph G., Deborah S. Franzblau, and Fred S. Roberts, eds. *Discrete Mathematics in the Schools*, Volume 36 of DIMACS Series in Discrete Mathematics and Theoretical Computer Science. Providence, RI: American Mathematical Society and the National Council of Teachers of Mathematics, 1997. A series of articles from a 1992 conference on how and why discrete mathematics can be taught in K-12 classrooms.

Tang, Greg. *The Grapes of Math*. Scholastic Press, 2001. Colorful picture book that asks kids to count the number of objects on each page by figuring out clever shortcuts. An excellent introduction to problem-solving strategies commonly used in discrete mathematics.

CHAPTER 2
Clap Your Name

Developing number sense through music

Grades	K-12
Time	15 — 60 minutes
Groups of	2
Materials	Last part requires unifix cubes, paper and pencil
Space	Does not need much space. Most of the activities can be done in chairs, but are preferable seated on the floor.
Concepts	Number sense, patterning, pulse or beat, rhythmic sense, and polyrhythms
Related Activities:	Chapter 5 *Threesies*, Chapter 6 *Watch Your p's and q's*

Rhythm, wrote the poet Langston Hughes, "...is related to the rhythms of the earth as it moves around the sun, and to the moon... [and to] those vaster rhythms of time and space and wonder beyond the reach of eye and mind." In musical rhythms we find delightful patterns; in human designs and natural arrangements we find inspiration for musical rhythms. The mathematics of rhythm can be complex, and the ways rhythms are used vary considerably from culture to culture; learning about rhythm is a wonderful way to expand one's appreciation for other cultures.

In our first math/dance performance, we have the audience play a rhythm clapping game: half the audience claps a three pattern and the other half claps a four at the same time, and we watch what happens. Bobby Summerhill, a second-grade teacher we worked with in Soquel, California, plays another rhythm game with her students. The students convert their names to rhythms by making each consonant into a handclap, and each vowel into a slap of the thighs. Then Summerhill calls on her students by playing the rhythm of their name. We decided to put these two activities together: two students will play their names at the same time, and we will create both enjoyable rhythms and a context for understanding the notion of the least common multiple.

2-1. Warm-up: Follow the Leader (1-3 minutes)

This warm-up works well with younger kids K-3. Older children and adults like it too.
- Perform a pattern by clapping your hands and slapping your thighs several times. For instance, one pattern might be CLAP-slap-slap-clap (and repeat, perhaps accenting the first clap).
- Have the class imitate in unison.
- Make up and perform another pattern and have the class imitate.

- Try longer patterns.
- Try putting pauses into your pattern. For instance, try clap-slap-pause-clap (repeat). Or slap-clap-pause (repeat).
- Make up additional patterns of your own.

2-2. Play your Name (10 minutes)

In this activity students translate the letters in their first names into clapping patterns.
- Have the students learn to sound out the letters of their first names by clapping their hands for a consonant and slapping their thighs for a vowel. For example, M-A-R-I-A would be played clap-slap-clap-slap-slap.
- Students with a Y in their names enjoy deciding for themselves whether their Y is a vowel or a consonant. When we visited Hawai'i we found that many younger students in the Hawai'ian language immersion program on Kaui'i played the "okina" or glottal stop (indicated by the apostrophe in the name Hawai'i, for example) as a consonant, because the okina actually is a consonant in the Hawi'ian language.
- Tell students, "Learn to play your name pattern without pauses, so every clap and slap takes the same amount of time." While there is nothing wrong with making some beats longer than others, and it can even be fun, this exercise works better if all beats are the same length. This is a great way to practice feeling a steady beat or groove.

Demonstrate
- Go around the room and have students demonstrate the rhythm of their names.
- Ask students, "Are any of the sequences the same? Why?"
- See if students are inserting pauses or playing some letters faster than others. Remind students that, although it is musically interesting to insert pauses or change speeds, for this exercise try to stay consistent.
- Ask the students if they can determine who might have the same sequence before they listen to the names?
- See if the students recognize their own patterns. If Bill is in the class, clap his name and see if he recognizes it. Of course, Jill might also raise her hand. Try clapping students' patterns several times.

2-3. Play the Names Three Times in a Row (5-10 minutes)

Repeating a name creates a pattern.
- Tell students, "Now try to play your name three times in a row, without pausing at the end of your name. Make sure every clap or slap lasts the same amount of time."
- Students often want to pause at the end of their name (M-A-R-I-A—M-A-R-I-A—). Have them practice going right back to the beginning (M-A-R-I-A-M-A-R-I-A). Again, for the purposes of this exercise, students should learn to clap out their names evenly.
- Have them accent the first letter of the name. For example, accenting the "M" in "Maria" creates a five beat pattern (M-a-r-i-a-M-a-r-i-a-M-a-r-i-a). To illustrate the concept, choose one name in the class that is easier (Abe or Lena for example) and have the whole class learn to accent the first letter together (A-b-e-A-b-e-A-b-e).
- Again have students demonstrate the rhythm of their names, played repeatedly. Ask the students to listen and decide whether each letter took the same amount of time.

Hints: Try not to pound. Keep the sounds audible but soft. Amid soft slapping and clapping, it is much easier (and less painful) to accent one sound if the rest of the sounds are soft. Replacing sounds: If the thigh slap or clap do not work for some students, encourage them to come up with their own. As long as the sound is fairly consistent, it will work. We have seen students slap the floor, vocalize on the first letter of their names, and more. Some students may have trouble because they attempt to play their names at too fast a tempo: encourage them to learn it at a slower tempo first!

2-4. Play your Name with a Partner (15-20 minutes)

In this activity, more complex rhythms are created by combining the patterns of two names.
- Have students pair up. The only requirement is that two students in a pair can not have the same number of letters in their names.
- Have each pair sit facing one other. Have them play their names at the same time, and at the same speed. For younger students, have the class try it once with two names. Choose two short names from the class (Sue and Juan, for example) and divide the class in half. Have one half learn to play Sue and the other learn to play Juan. It helps to have leaders of each half who have a solid sense of rhythm. Have the class play Sue and Juan at the same time. Then have the class return to their pairs and try.
- Remind students, "Try not to get confused by listening too closely (at first) to what the other person is doing. Do not speed up or slow down; a steady beat allows each of you to continue playing without getting confused."
- Allow time for students to practice. This exercise can be tricky, especially for those with long names. We have found that in a group there will be a range of abilities: some struggle just to play their names alone, others are challenged by putting two names together, and others still can play two names easily and musically. Encourage and help, but there is no need to insist.
- After the students practice awhile, have several groups demonstrate. They may need to demonstrate several times in order to get it right.

2-5. Look at the Mathematics of the Combined Rhythms (10-15 minutes)

In this activity, questions are posed about the rhythms students just worked on.

- Ask the students the following questions: Do any of the paired names produce particularly pleasing rhythms? Why or why not?
- Can any pair play their names until they get back to the beginning: that is, the accented first letters meet up? After how many beats will the accented letters coincide? For example, two names of lengths 4 and 6 letters will coincide after 12 beats, 12 being the "least common multiple" of 4 and 6. Let students discover an answer by experimenting. Have a pair of students demonstrate, so everyone can listen for the accented beats coming together.

For example, here is what happens when Teri and Thomas play their names together:

Beat:	1	2	3	4	5	6	7	8	9	10	11	12	13
Teri	T	e	r	i	T	e	r	i	T	e	r	i	T
Thomas	T	h	o	m	a	s	T	h	o	m	a	s	T

- Notice that beats 1 and 13, at which both T's are played loudly, are separated by 12 beats. 12 is the smallest number that is made up of an even number of 4's and also an even number of 6's; we say it is the least common multiple of 4 and 6.

Write down the patterns
- Hand out paper and colored pens or crayons and ask students, "Make up a way to write down your rhythm. Can you make a picture out of your rhythm?" Do not ask or expect students to use conventional musical notation; the process of inventing their own notation is valuable. We have had students arrange the names

in lines, as in the diagram for Teri and Thomas above. We have seen students arrange names in circles, use colors or capital letters or geometric shapes to indicate accents.
- Once they have notated their rhythms, ask them, "Can you read your rhythm and use your picture as a 'score' to remind you how to play different names?"
- Ask students if they can teach someone else how to play their picture or notation. This exercise is a natural bridge to abstract symbol systems like algebra. It helps students realize that all symbol systems — the alphabet, mathematical symbols, musical notation — are invented by people.
- Display the rhythm pictures as visual art, and get feedback from other students.

2-6. Make a Dance from the Patterns (10-15 minutes)

In this activity, students extend their name patterns into movement patterns. Students first work individually, then they return to their pairs.
- Have the students stand. Have the class move slowly until you say "freeze!" Remind them that wherever they are when you say "freeze," that is where they must stop. Have the class wiggle until you say "freeze!" Make up your own words and repeat the exercise, or have the class suggest ways of moving.
- Tell students, "I want each of you to make up one movement on your own. It can be slow or fast, big or little, high or low, smooth or jerky. You can do something you saw somebody do today, or you can just move the way you feel. But remember, it needs to be one movement with a clear beginning and a clear ending."
- Have the students demonstrate their movements individually. If they are shy, three or four can demonstrate at the same time. If it seems students are unsure of their movements, have them repeat the movements. It is important that each student know the movement thoroughly and can repeat it accurately. After demonstrating, if the students are not moving clearly, have them work on the movements and demonstrate again.
- Have students return to their pairs. Tell students, "Now each pair has two movements, one for each member of the pair. Teach one another your movements. Practice them so that you can do them the same." We have found that sometimes students simplify or reduce the level of energy of a movement when they teach. Go around the room and encourage students to preserve the energy and individuality of the movements they are learning.
- When the pairs know their movements, have the students assign one movement from the pair to be a consonant, the other movement to be a vowel. Then have them perform the movements according to the pattern of one of their names. For instance, a clap might become a step, and a slap a kick. So J-E-N-N-I would become step-kick-step-step-kick. In this case, the steps will alternate feet, which complicates things a bit more.
- Slowing the rhythm down may help, since clapping and slapping can be done much faster than walking, for example. Also, two movements do not always fit together easily, in which case the students in the pair will have to make a simple transition between movements. The really ambitious may try doing the movement sequences for two names at the same time — as they did with the clapping patterns.
- Have the partners demonstrate their movement phrases. Have students give feedback for each pair — what did the phrases look like when taken into movement? What was interesting or enjoyable about each pair's choices or performance? Which was harder, clapping by oneself or clapping with a partner? Why? Did it get easier? Was it fun to listen to other people's rhythms? Who was good at it and why? Were there any tricks that made it easier?

2-7. Asessment and Reflection

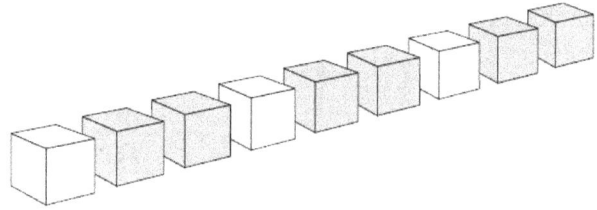

- Were students able to play their names? Did the clarity of the patterns and the steadiness of the pulse improve with practice?
- Were students able to play their own names repeatedly, without placing a pause at the end of the name (those with names of length 7 or 5 may be more tempted to add this silent paused beat, since 8's and 6's are common in popular music). Not all students will be able to play their name patterns against their parters' names. Even if they were not able to do this, did they understand how to practice, by slowing down and keeping the same beat as their partners?
- Were students able to create a short movement that was clear? Were students able to learn their partners' movements? Were they able to link the two movements in a sequence? Did they need to create transitions between the movements, and if so, were they successful?
- Were they able to calculate the length of the rhythm created by joining two names of different lengths?
- Were they able to notate their combined rhythms in a consistent manner?

Some Common Confusions

Least Common Multiple
One of the concepts clarified in this section is that of least common multiple: what is the smallest number of total beats after which two rhythms played simultaneously start together again? We found that the smallest repeating pattern for names of length 4 and 6 is not their product 24, but 12, since 12 is a smaller multiple of both 4 and 6. Sometimes students insist that we should add the two numbers, 4 and 6, to get 10, and that should be the smallest repeating block. It is important to clarify that we are looking for a number that will be an even number of groups of each name, and that means it must be a multiple of each.

In some cases we actually do multiply the numbers together to get the least common multiple (when the numbers have no factors in common, for example with names of length 3 and 4). Students may say that the reason the names repeat after 12 beats is that "12 is 3 times 4." Ask for more explanation: "Why do we multiply in this case, whereas multiplication does not work with 4 and 6?" For that matter, ask for an explanation of why we multiply rather than add — this gets to the basic idea that multiplication is the operation that calculates the result of putting equal groups together.

Fence post problem
Another confusion sometimes arises in the counting process itself. For example, here are two names of length 4 and 6 played together:

Beat:	1	2	3	4	5	6	7	8	9	10	11	12	13
Mary	M	a	r	y	M	a	r	y	M	a	r	y	M
Thomas	T	h	o	m	a	s	T	h	o	m	a	s	T

Even though the accented first letters occur together again at beat 13, the repeating block of the rhythm is only 12 beats long. We do not want to count both beat 1 and beat 13 as part of that block. Sometimes students will say that the rhythm repeats after 13 beats, not 12. This is an example of what is sometimes called the "fence post problem": a fence that is 12 fence rails in length requires 13 fence posts:

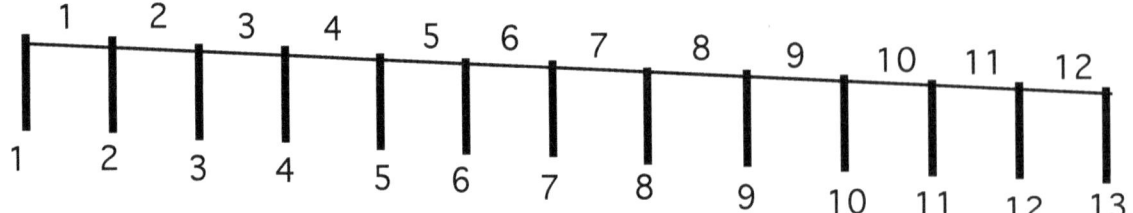

However in music and dance we are more concerned with the length of the block of sounds or movement that one performer must repeat, not with the number of markers delineating that block.

2-8. Further Activities

Dancing two patterns at once. In section 2-6, pairs of students made two movements, assigned one to consonant and the other to vowel, then made dances from the clapping patterns, and danced them together. As an extra challenge, see if the students can dance the patterns of their names at the same time. In other words, this exercise is a dancing version of the clapping exercise where pairs of students clapped names of different lengths at the same time. When the students try to dance their names patterns, are those patterns clear visually? What is the difference between seeing a pattern and hearing one? Another challenge is to have students make their consonant movements travel, while leaving the vowel patterns stationary. What does the resulting dance look like? Does it make the patterns more visible? Is it harder to keep the rhythm while traveling?

Three names at once. If a pair of students is able to clap two names of different lengths at the same time and come up with a new rhythm, do you think three students could do this? To start, try to find three names of different lengths that are not too long (for example Bob, Pina and Steven). Before the students perform the rhythm, can the class figure out how many times each person would have to play their name before all the first letters matched up?

Clapping is music. The composer Steve Reich, termed by some a minimalist composer, has made beautiful pieces of music that are made up of only hand clapping patterns. Flamenco dancers have to be able to do palmas, that is, clapping patterns to accompany the dancers. There are also traditional American forms that involve clapping, slapping and other limb-produced sounds, such at Stepping or Hambone. Research these or other forms and try to make up a piece of music/dance that uses those techniques.

Playing with rhythm
- Use Unifix cubes or other colored objects to make visual patterns. Try using more than two kinds of sounds. For example, red might stand for clap, blue for slap thighs, green for snap fingers.
- Try accenting other beats besides the first letter of each name.
- Try putting more than two names together.
- Try different arrangements of the cubes: lines, circles, left to right, top to bottom, back and forth. Arrange cubes in different patterns and attempt to clap-slap out the rhythm.
- A metronome might help students keep a steady rhythm.
- Have students find rhythms around them, in pictures, patterns, or words they really like. Have them play the rhythms and show everyone the pictures or sources for their rhythms.
- Ask them if they can find the rhythms of their names somewhere else, in a picture, a tree, a clothing design or some other object.

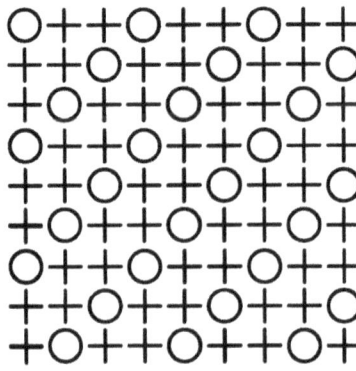

Find rhythmic patterns in popular and world music
- Ask the students to find music exhibiting rhythms of lengths other than 4 or 8. If the teacher is not comfortable counting music, consult with a musician or music teacher or dance teacher.
- Investigate music from other cultures. Non-western music often uses more complex rhythmic structures than does the popular music heard on the radio in this country.
- Find folk dances built on unusual rhythms. Learn and perform them for class, or watch them on video.
- Find examples of unusual rhythms in popular music. Two well-known pieces in 5 are theme from *Mission Impossible* and Dave Brubeck's jazz composition *Take Five*. See the references at the end of this chapter for other music in unusual meter.

Poinsot Stars

We might also look more closely at how two rhythms interact. For example, here is a diagram showing how the accented first letter of the three-letter name Syd falls with respect to a five letter name Marin:

Beat:	1	2	3	4	5	6	7	8	9	10	11	12	13	14	15	16
Marin	**M**	a	r	i	n	**M**	a	r	i	n	**M**	a	r	i	n	**M**
Syd	**S**	y	d	**S**	y	d	**S**	y	d	**S**	y	d	**S**	y	d	**S**

Notice that the S in Syd falls first opposite the M, then the i, than the a, then the n, then the r, and finally returns to the M. If we draw this pattern as a circular diagram (start at the S just at the top of the circle), we can see that the S in Syd traverses a beautiful five-pointed star within the circle for Marin:

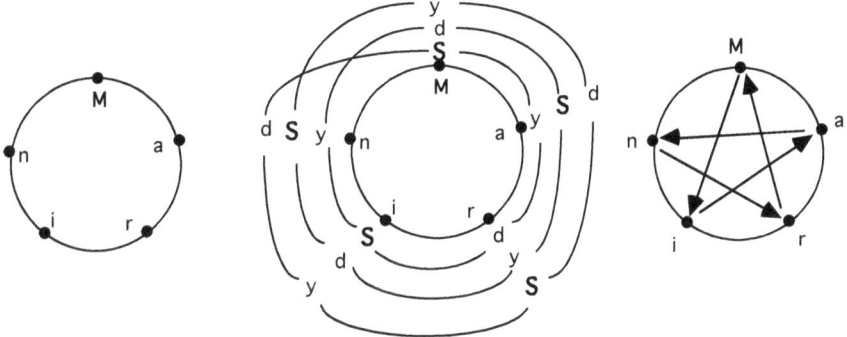

This is an example of what is sometimes called a Poinsot star, after a French mathematician who studied them in 1809. These circular patterns are also found in artwork and symbology from a variety of cultures.
- Students may wish to draw their rhythm patterns in this way, and see what stars their names create.
- Investigate which pairs of names have the property that the accented first letter of each name appears at some time opposite every letter of the other name. What does this have to do with how we calculate the least common multiple?
- Investigate the way that accented first letters of names which differ in length by one letter seem to cycle away from each other, and then return. For example, Kristy and Marti exhibit this effect. The class might listen for this pattern when the names are played, as well as observe it in the diagrams.

1	2	3	4	5	6	7	8	9	10	11	12	13	14	15	16	17	18	19	20	21	22	23	24	25	26	27	28	29	30	31
K	r	i	s	t	y	**K**	r	i	s	t	y	**K**	r	i	s	t	y	**K**	r	i	s	t	y	**K**	r	i	s	t	y	**K**
M	a	r	t	i	**M**	a	r	t	i	**M**	a	r	t	i	**M**	a	r	t	i	**M**	a	r	t	i	**M**	a	r	t	i	**M**

A Puzzle

The following chart shows a portion of the pattern of the loud sounds (*) when two names were played together. Can you figure out how long the names are:

*		*	*			*	*		*			*			*		*

2-7. Resources

http://www.folkdancing.org/. Maintains a 120 page folk dance site, including a large U.S./Canada directory of folk dance groups and teachers.

Flatishhler, Reinhard. *The Forgotten Power of Rhythm*. Mendocino, CA: LifeRhythm, 1992. Essay on the use of rhythm in world music.

Hirsch, Christian R. "Poinsot Stars," Activities from the Mathematics Teacher, ed. by Evan M. Maletsky and Christian R. Hirsch. Reston, VA: National Council of Teachers of Mathematics, 1981. Classroom activities involving Poinsot stars, from a January 1980 issue of the Mathematics Teacher, also published by the NCTM.

Hughes, Langston. *The Book of Rhythms*. New York: Oxford University Press, 1995. Originally published as *The first book of rhythms*, New York: F. Watts, 1954. A delightful exploration of rhythm in language, art and life, and a good source for movement ideas.

Jamison, Robert E. "Rhythm and Pattern: Discrete Mathematics with an Artistic Connection for Elementary School Teachers," *Discrete Mathematics in the Schools,* ed. by Rosenstein, Joseph G., Deborah S. Franzblau, Fred.S. Roberts. DIMACS Series in Discrete Mathematics and Theoretical Compute Science, Vol. 36., publ. by American Mathematical Society, 1997, pp 203-222. An overview of how symmetry activities and the arts may be used in teaching mathematics. Movement ideas inspired by the movement form eurythmy, taught in the Waldorf Schools.

Thie, Joseph A. *Rhythm and Dance Mathematics*,. Minneapolis: published by Joseph Thie, 1964 (once available from the Dance Mart, Box 48, Brooklyn, NY 11229.) Applies the mathematical technique known as correlation analysis to sequences of dance steps. Includes some analysis of dance and mathematics with a larger scope. This book is available in the Lincoln Center Library and in the Dance Collection of the Birmingham Public Library, in Birmingham, Alabama.

Music
All You Need is Love by The Beatles. Alternates between 7 and 8 beat phrases.

The Dave Brubeck Quartet — Time Out, Columbia Records CK 40585. In addition to the five beat jazz classic "Take Five," composed by Paul Desmond, this album contains Dave Brubeck's compositions in unusual meters, including 9 beat, 10 beat and even fourteen beat patterns.

Pink Floyd's *Money*.

Mission Accomplished: Themes for Spies and Cops, MCA Special Markets and products, Inc. HPO 40017, 1996. Contains Lalo Schifrin's theme for Mission: Impossible, composed to a five beat rhythm.

Stravinsky's *Rite of Spring*. Contains many complex rhythms, often simultaneously.

CHAPTER 3
Heads or Tails?
Making sense of uncertainty through chance in dance

Grades:	3-12
Time:	20-60 minutes
Groups:	Entire class, groups of 2-5
Concepts:	Math: Probability
	Dance: Chance in choreography, transitions, pattern recognition and memory
Space:	Cleared classroom; some activities are better in a gym
Materials:	Pencil and paper
Related Activities:	Chapter 1 *How Many Ways to Shake Hands* and Chapter 2 *Clap Your Name*

We all use expressions like "probably" or "in all likelihood." Translating an intuitive understanding of probability into precise terms, however, takes work. It was not until the mid-17th century that Pascal and Fermat began formalizing the mathematics of probability. Dancers, artists, writers and musicians began working extensively with probability only in the mid-20th century.

In this chapter students toss coins and record the sequences of heads and tails. These sequences are translated into movement patterns, and students are asked to look carefully at the results.

When we first taught these exercises, it became clear that learning phrases of movement that are dictated by coin tosses makes the dry results of probability far more memorable. We also found that performing the phrases poses coordination challenges, and invites students to investigate the transitions between movements.

The movement sequences become palpable objects for the students to refer to as they discuss and observe the rules of probability. Students then gain an understanding and appreciation of the patterns to be found in seemingly arbitrary results. The resulting dance phrases are often wonderfully surprising.

3-1. Getting Started (3-5 minutes)

Start with a discussion question.
- Ask your students "What is probability?"
- We encourage you to let the students say whatever comes to mind, so they at least start to clarify what they think probability is. Write down some of the statements students make. Do not correct their answers at this point. This question will be posed again at the end of the chapter. We have heard such varied responses as: "Chance," "You can't tell what the coin will be," or "Just guessing."

3-2. Coin Toss (7-15 minutes)

In this activity, students flip coins and record the outcomes. The results serve as a springboard for discussions about probability.
- In front of the class, have one student flip a coin twenty times and another student record the number of heads and tails that come up on a chalkboard.
- Have all of the students pair up and flip a coin five times and record the results. Display some of the results. Normally, some of the five tosses will be more skewed towards all heads or all tails than will the twenty tosses.

- Here are two examples of each toss:

  Five tosses: Twenty tosses:
  5 heads, 0 tails   9 heads, 11 tails
  2 heads, 3 tails   12 heads, 8 tails

- Ask the students, "If we tossed the coin one hundred times, what do you think the results would be? "
- "If we flipped a coin 99 times and it came up heads every time, what is the probability that it would come up heads again if we flip it for the 100th time? " Some students will argue for heads, since this will continue the pattern. Some students will argue for tails since it seems to them to be getting more and more likely that the pattern will break. Both of these are common psychological traps that people fall into when playing games of chance. The mathematical theory of probability is based on the principle that the outcome of each flip is completely independent of all other flips. So it does not matter what has happened before — the probability of a 100th head remains 50%. On the other hand 99 consecutive heads is strong evidence that the coin is unfairly biased towards heads!

> **Math Note: Flipping a Coin**
> There are two possible outcomes when we throw a coin (unless you count the unlikely event of the coin standing on edge). We usually assume heads and tails are equally likely, though it is of interest that during World War II the scientist John Kerrich, imprisoned by the Nazis, spent much of his time testing this hypothesis by throwing a coin thousands of times. He found heads occurring 50.7% of the time in a test of 10,000 tosses. For these exercises please assume that heads and tails each occur 50% of the time!

3-3. Create a Class Sequence (5-10 minutes)

In this activity a random sequence of coin tosses is turned into a corresponding sequence of movements.
- To warm up, have students move their arms in big circular motions. Have them start slowly, and gradually get more vigorous. First left, then right.
- Have students do the same thing with their legs.
- Ask students, "What is the opposite of 'circular?'" As there is not one right answer, have students experiment and try a variety of options first with their arms and then legs.
- Explain to students, "For today, a movement is something that has a clear beginning and a clear ending. It can be fast or slow, sudden or smooth or jerky, but the start and finish must be clear." Have students try making up a movement. As a class, look at some movements in terms of their clarity and definition.
- As a class, pick two movements from the students' creations and assign one movement to "Heads" and the other to "Tails." Two approaches to choosing the movements that we have used are: 1) choose the class's two favorite movements from the exercise they just did; or, 2) pick the two most contrasting movements.
- Take the two movements the class just selected and assign one to heads, another to tails. As a class, toss a coin five times, and try the resulting sequence of movements. Have the whole class practice the phrase. If time allows, see if they can do it together as an ensemble. Remember, just about any movement is fair game: a gesture, a jump, a turn, moving to a shape, a wiggle, moving the eyebrows, etc.

Example: In one class we taught, the movements the class chose were
   1) putting the right hand over the face and
   2) jumping up and tucking the legs

The sequence of five coin tosses came up Heads, Tails, Heads, Heads, Tails. The class assigned "Heads" to movement # 1 and "Tails" to movement # 2.

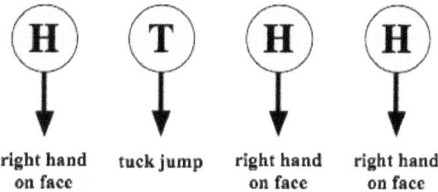

In this particular phrase, some students tended to Tuck Jump before the Right Hand On Face movement was complete. For the class to be together they decided to make sure the Right Hand On Face movement was complete and the right arm was at their sides before they went on to the jump. This is one example of the decisions that are necessary when putting phrases together.

Dance Note: Probability in Art
In the twentieth century, at least, probability and the arts have often overlapped. Writers, composers, and performers have consciously used chance to make artistic choices. As a research project, students might study John Cage, Brian Eno, Merce Cunningham, William Burroughs and many others. Scientific ideas, as well as the I Ching and other ideas from non-Western cultures, influenced the work of these and many other artists. Their use of chance was considered radical at the time. What traditional ideas in art were challenged by this new approach to the creative process? In particular, what role does artistic-choice play in these two approaches?

3-4. Create Sequences in Smaller Groups (7-15 minutes)

In this activity students pair up and create random sequences of their own. If time is short, the class might use movements from the previous section to make sequences. In that case, skip over "Make up movements" and "Combine movements" and go directly to "Make random sequences" below.

Make up movements
Have each student work individually. Ask the class to:
- Make up a brief movement with the arms or the legs (Ideally, these should be different from the movements created in the section 3-3).
- Make up a jump they like.
- Do a gesture they noticed someone doing that day.
- Make up any movement they want.

Combine movements
- Each student chooses one of the four movements (for younger students) or combines two of these four movements (for students who need a challenge).
- When combining, see if the students can do them at the same time as opposed to sequentially. For example, do the arm movement while jumping.
- The only restriction is it must be clear where the statement begins and ends. Remind students that they must be able to repeat the movement consistently, clearly and with energy.

Make random sequences
- Have students pair up and teach each other their movements.
- Make sure each pair has a coin. Have each pair assign one of their movements to Heads, another to Tails. They then toss the coin five times and create a movement sequence.

- If time allows, have pairs perform their sequences. As is often the case, transitions (from one movement to the next, or even from one movement to the same movement) can be tricky. Encourage students to find clear and creative solutions to transition problems.
- If time allows, have students discuss how it looked. Add music.

> **Dance Note: Preserving Idiosyncracies**
>
> Sometimes in the process of teaching their movements, students simplify or remove the interesting idiosyncrasies. Encourage them to preserve, or even solidify, those idiosyncrasies rather than let them disappear. The individual ways students express themselves physically are what make each movement unique! We often suggest that students simply demonstrate the movements clearly and have the partners try to imitate, rather than explaining in detail the movements.

3-5. More Coins, More Movements (7-15 minutes)

Students have just used one coin to choose between two movements. But what if they wanted to create a sequence using three or four or even five movements? How could this be done? One way is to toss more than one coin at a time. Tossing two coins, however, increases the complexity.

In this activity, students look at the outcomes and probabilities when flipping two coins. To get a feel for the outcomes, do another trial run in front of the whole class.

- Designate two students as the tossers, giving each one coin. A third student is the recorder. The two tossers toss at the same time and report the results.
- Have the students try twenty tosses (each tosser tosses twenty times).
- At this point, either discuss with students the chart below, or continue on to section 3-6.
- At first glance you may decide that there are **three** outcomes: two heads, two tails, and one of each. But are these three outcomes equally likely to occur?
- Out of the twenty tosses, are they almost evenly divided between three or four possible outcomes?

It could also be looked at as **four** outcomes. To show why this is the case we sometimes tabulate the possibilities in the form of a tree:

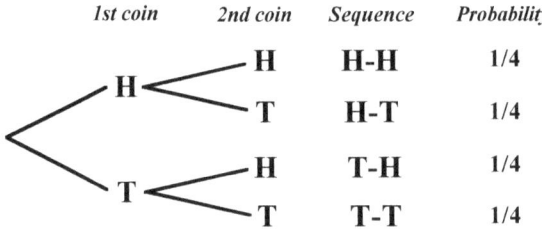

This chart operates on the principle that one head and one tail occur 50% of the time, on average. The combination of heads and tails occurs twice (H-T, and T-H). In other words, 1/4 of the tosses will be H-T, and 1/4 of the tosses will be T-H. So some combinations of heads and tails will occur half of the time (1/4+1/4=1/2).

In the class we taught, they chose to keep their first two movements (mentioned in section 3-3) and for their third movement they chose a full-body wiggle. So their three movements were:
1. hand to face
2. jump-tuck
3. wiggle

The class chose to assign the full-body wiggle to any head-tail combination, the hand to face movement to T-T and the jump-tuck to H-H. We asked the class, "which movement is likely to occur most often?" The students decided that the wiggle was likely to occur most often, because either a head-tail or tail-head combination signals that movement. In a test of ten coin tosses, the wiggle came up five times, the jump-tuck four and the hand to face once.

Remember, the above example is just one way to do it. There a many other approaches: tossing coins separately, using three coins, tossing only one coin twice in a row, and so on.

3-6. Devising Ways To Select Movements (5-10 minutes)

There are many other ways to generate random choices. Which ones are fair, treating all choices equally?
- Using two or three coins, have students invent a method to choose between **three to five** possible movements. Remind them that they do not have to use the example described in the previous section. Ask them if their methods make all the movements equally likely, or will the ratio be skewed? This exercise requires that students make up more movements.
- Using the methods students just devised for choosing between three to five movements, have them create sequences of these movements by tossing coins.
- Ask the students if they found themselves doing certain movements more frequently than others. Ask them to explain the difference in rates of occurrence.

> **Math note: Random numbers from an almanac**
> One way to generate a random number between 1 and 9 is to choose the first digit of a number chosen randomly from the street addresses listed in the phone book, or from an almanac, which lists things like populations of cities, areas of lakes and so on. (If you want to choose a random number in a smaller range, say between 1 and 6, you can use the same procedure but discard choices between 7 and 9.) If you try this, however, you will discover that the number 1 occurs nearly 1/3 of the time, with other choices 2-9 occurring less and less frequently. This is because the leading digits of physical measurements are not evenly distributed among the numbers 1 through 9. As numbers increase the number of objects with those numbers tend to decrease. Bigger population numbers correspond to fewer cities. The leading digits of most of nature's or humanity's measurements seem to trail off in a manner that follows a logarithmic distribution law, known as Benford's law or the first digit phenomenon. This law has been used to detect fraud in business, when culprits fail to create false data that follow the law!

3-7. Reflection & Assessment

The Dance
Have students discuss the following:
- "What did you discover? Did the use of chance constructions encourage you to move in novel ways?"
- "What if you tried to create a dance using dice? How would it work?"
- Brainstorm on different ways to use chance to make choices.
- How were transitions handled? What were some of the ways of devising transitions from one movement to another?
- "If you used chance to compose a dance, can you legitimately be called the creator of the dance?"
- What are the benefits of using chance in dance? What are the drawbacks?
- How is chance used in today's music, movies, art, books, games or other arts?

After the groups of students have demonstrated their sequences, have them practice so they can do them clearly and with energy. If one group of students comes up with a particularly fun sequence, have everyone learn it and perform it as a class.

In assessing the students, ask the following questions about their work:
- Did the clarity of the dancing increase with practice?
- Did the dance phrase include the ideas we were working with?

- Did they commit to creating and working on the dances?
- Did the students perform fully or were they hesitant? If they were hesitant, how might the general atmosphere in the class be improved to help students feel more comfortable?
- Were the properties of chance explored? Did the students make good choices in assigning movements?
- Were they able to make deductions based on the effects of probability?

The Math

Definitions, again. Ask the class the question that began this chapter: "What is probability? " See if the answers include rules or tendencies gleaned from the activities. One of the confusing things about probability is that it does not usually predict what will actually happen the next time, it calculates the likelihood that something will happen. The patterns of probability become more and more visible as the number of trials increase.

Recognizing Probability. Take time as a class to watch some or all of the movement phrases that the different groups invented. Using what students have learned about probability, ask if they can now make inferences from the phrase(s)? How many movements are used? Is it possible to guess how the coin tosses generated the movement? For example, if there are three movements, but one occurs more than the other two, ask the class why they think this happened. Have students describe in writing the process by which they assigned movements to tosses. Have students compare the notes with those of other groups. Are the notes similar or different? As a class, try to devise a system to describe probability.

More coins, more questions. When you toss two coins you have four possible outcomes — H-H, H-T, T-H, T-T — or $2^2 = 4$. With three coins we get $2^3 = 8$ possible outcomes, each occurring 1/8th of the time:

1st coin	2nd coin	3rd coin	Sequence	Probability
H	H	H	H-H-H	1/8
H	H	T	H-H-T	1/8
H	T	H	H-T-H	1/8
H	T	T	H-T-T	1/8
T	H	H	T-H-H	1/8
T	H	T	T-H-T	1/8
T	T	H	T-T-H	1/8
T	T	T	T-T-T	1/8

We can ask many questions about this diagram. The questions can be answered theoretically by studying the diagram, or experimentally, by throwing three coins a number of times and tabulating the results.
- What is the probability that there will be more heads than tails when we toss 3 coins at once?
- What is the probability of getting two heads and one tail when we toss 3 coins at once?
- What is the probability that all coins will be the same when we toss 3 coins at once?
- Suppose we color one of the three coins red. What is the probability that the red coin will come up heads when we toss 3 coins at once?
- What is the probability that the number of heads and tails will be the same when we toss 4 coins at once? 6 coins? 10 coins? 99 coins?
- What is the most likely number of heads and tails if we toss 10 coins at once? 11 coins?
- Suppose we keep throwing a coin until it comes up heads. For instance we might throw it once and it may come up heads. Or three times and it comes up tails, tails, heads. On average, how many times must we throw it until it produce heads for the first time?
- If we throw a pair of dice, what is the probability of rolling a 7? 11? Which is more likely, 11 or 12?

> **Math Note: Penny Pinching**
> If we balance a penny on its edge on a table, then strike the table sharply, what is the probability that it will come to rest heads? What is the probability that it will come up tails? Try it! The mathematician John Conway is fond of this question because, as it turns out, the edge of a penny is not perpendicular to its surface. Why? It would be extremely difficult to pull the newly minted pennies out of their molds, so the edge of a penny is angled slightly to allow it to fall out of the mold. This affects the way a balanced penny will fall. What about if you spin the penny on its edge? Will the outcome be different from hitting the table? Conway likes to use these effects to try to convince colleagues that he has the power to make coins fall any way he likes.

3-8. Further Activities

Make a Dance. Have students put aside probability and look at the phrases. Ask students what they like, what they don't like, what areas seem to need more development. With the students make a list of things to do to change or extend the movement. Examples of variations:
- Have the groups travel as they do their sequences.
- Since the sequences are probably brief, make variations on the phrases so that they can be repeated.
- Have groups play with not being in unison.
- Put two groups together in some way.

Oblique Strategies. The contemporary composer/producer Brian Eno created a deck of cards called Oblique Strategies, on which he wrote open-ended suggestions, such as "Go Back To The Beginning" or "Honor Your Mistakes As Hidden Intentions." When he got stuck in the composing process, he would choose a card at random and use the statement on it to guide him towards a decision. In making their dances, can students create a deck of similar cards? Have each student try to write one open-ended suggestion, and create a class deck.

Traffic Patterns. Probability and mathematics associated with probability are used in many fields. Traffic patterns are subject to the laws of probability. Make a study of how probability is used for traffic flow in the students' area. Can the rules you discover be used for anything else, such as foot traffic at school?

3-9. Resources

Ekeland, Ivars. *The Broken Dice and Other Mathematical Tales of Chance.*

Eno, Brian and Peter Schmidt. *Oblique Strategies.* Originally privately printed in 1975. A deck of 100 creative suggestions like "Don't be frightened of clichés" to inspire artists and musicians. Available on the web at http://www.rtqe.net/ObliqueStrategies/

Peterson, Ivars. *The Jungles of Randomness: A Mathematical Safari.* New York: John Wiley and Sons, 1998. Readable account of contemporary views of chance and randomness.

Peterson, Ivars. "First Digits," at http://www.sciencenews.org/Sn_arc98/6_27_98/mathland.htm, *Science News Online, June 27, 1998.* Brief summary of the first digit phenomenon, the tendency for constants from nature to have first digit one more often than any other.

Von Oech, Roger. *The Creative Whack Pack.* A deck of 64 random creative problem solving strategies Available on the web at http://www.creativethink.com.

CHAPTER 4
The Incredible Expanding Path
From lines on paper to paths in space

Grades:	K–12
Time:	20-60 minutes
Concepts:	Math: Scale, shape, estimation
	Dance: Scale, shapes, mechanics of how the body travels
Groups of:	solo, 2-5
Space:	A large open room, such as a gym or multi-purpose room.
Materials:	Paper and pencil (optional: unifix cubes)
Related activities:	Chapter 11 *Moving with Giant Tangrams* and chapter 12 *Storytelling with Giant Tangrams* both involve translating patterns between small and large scales

What makes a person good at reading maps? A map reader must be able to look at the lines and shapes on paper and imagine them greatly expanded. Of course, the adept map reader must also be able to do the inverse: look at a large area (a mountain range, a zoo, a grid of streets, etc.) and create a smaller mental picture of that area. Of equal importance, the map reader must imagine that large area as seen from above. These mental manipulations require practice.

In this chapter, students take shapes drawn on paper, increase the scale of those shapes, and "draw" them on the floor. Initially, the spatial paths on the floor are described by walking or running. Then students travel in more unusual ways. The spatial paths should be as big as the room in which students are dancing.

When we first taught this exercise, it vividly brought to our attention that dancers must think about the movements they are doing at the same time they are thinking about where they are on stage, and where they are in relation to other moving bodies. The following exercises help students strengthen this "outside eye" and learn mathematical ways of checking relative size.

> **Dance note: Floor patterns**
> Square dance, May Pole dance, whirling dervish: the names themselves conjure images of spatial arrangements and patterns. From contra dance, in which lines of dancers intertwine, to the disco era hustle, to the elaborate structure of the waltz which strictly guides when and how men and women join and separate, spatial paths and patterns have as much to do with some dances as the individual movements made by the dancers. Many choreographers see the stage as a grid (much like the x and y axis used to plot mathematical formulas) onto which patterns can be superimposed.

4-1. Warm-up (5-10 minutes)

Make sure the dance area is free from dangerous objects on the floor or protruding into the space. Though traveling is fun, it poses a few risks, such as running into tables, other dancers, or obstructions. You want students to release energy, but do so safely.

These warm-up exercises get students to expand familiar shapes. For older students, many of these warm-ups might be skipped.

- Have the students form a circle. Then ask, "Is this an accurate circle?" If students notice the circle is not accurate, ask them "How can we fix it?"
- Tell students: "Using your finger, write your name in the air. Write it small, then bigger, then as big as you can. Write with your knee, elbow, nose, etc. Remember to draw as big as you can!"
- Have the students walk the shape of the first letter of their name. Challenge students to make the single letter fill up the room.

- Have individual students demonstrate their letters. Ask the class, "Does it look like the letter? What could they do to make it more clear?"
- Have one student draw a spatial path on a large piece of paper. The only rule is that the students must not take the pen off the paper; the drawing must be continuous. Ask for a volunteer to try to run according to the spatial path that was drawn.
- Repeat the process with different students.

4-2. Locomotion (5-10 minutes)

"Locus" means "place", and "motio" is the root of "motion." These activities get students to discover new ways to locomote other than walking and running. Traveling through the space can be very challenging; keep this in mind when observing the students. It often takes slow careful practice to become adept at some ways of traveling.

- Ask the students: "Can you walk backwards? Sideways? Make sure you are looking where you are going! Can you change from walking forward to sideways and backward? How slowly can you travel? As you feel more comfortable, gradually speed up. Can you move by pulling yourself with your arms? Can you hop, jump or skip across the room? Walk stiff-legged? Roll? Can you lift your legs high as you move? Can you walk and then roll?" NOTE: "Freeze" is a helpful word if the class gets too excited. Have them move slowly at first. Encourage them to devise their own ways of moving.
- Choose two points in the room and mark them with two simple items, such as shoes or chairs. Ask the students: "How many different ways do you think there are to get from one point to the other?" Brainstorm with the class. As ideas arise, have the students demonstrate or verbalize their ideas. The students' answers might take different forms: moving in a straight line, following a round-about path, crawling or running, dragging another student, playing leapfrog, pretending that a magnet is pulling one, moving as quietly as possible, picking interesting words such as "watery," "crab-like," or "explosive" to emulate.
- Collect the ideas about traveling from one point to another. Keep in mind that literal words, such as "monkey" or "car" sometimes lead more to pantomime (as in pretending to have hands on a steering wheel and running around the room) and less to movement exploration. The point of the exercise is not to make movements which allow an audience (the other students) to be able to guess what the mover is trying to be; the purpose is to find different ways to travel, to move through the space.
- Using the list of ideas about traveling, have each student find an individual way of moving through the space. This individual way of traveling can be very repetitious (step-jump-step-jump); or it can have many parts (roll-run-hop-slide—roll-run-hop-slide).
- Ask the students to remember their particular ways of locomoting for later use.

Dance note: Do you know where your center is?
Teachers of dance forms such as ballet, modern, jazz and African often refer to "the center." Tai Chi and other martial art forms refer to the tan t'ien, or hara, which is considered both the physical center and the center of energy. Anatomically speaking, the center is the point in the body which is the center of gravity when a person stands normally (the center of gravity may actually lie outside the body when we bend over!). It is usually somewhere in the middle of the body, slightly below the belly button (although this differs greatly from person to person). Dancers and martial artists also try to become aware of the center as the place out of which movement radiates. As you walk, dance, tumble or play a sport, try to become aware of where your center is and what it is doing. Or watch people as they walk. What part of the body do they lead with? Is there wasted effort in the walking? Any efficient movement requires efficient use of the center.

4-3. Expanding Paths (7-15 minutes)

From drawing to dancing. In this activity students take patterns on paper, expand them mentally, then dance those patterns in such a way that they occupy the entire floor. Older students might skip some steps.
- Have each student draw a spatial path on a separate sheet of paper. The pencil should not leave the paper while tracing a path. Remind students that simpler is better. Two or three turns in a path are plenty. Complicated paths may take too long to learn.
- Collect all the papers and redistribute them at random so each student receives another student's path.
- Encourage students to look carefully at their patterns. Ask them: "Are there curves in your pattern? Straight lines? Do the lines ever cross over each other? Are there parts of the pattern that are tight so that the lines are near one another? Are there parts that are more spread out? Does the pattern remind you of any geometric shapes?"
- Have the students trace their paths on the paper with their fingers. Then have the students try to trace them in the air. See if they can close their eyes and picture the paths. Ask the class to stand and look around the room. Ask them, "Without moving, can you picture your path expanded so big that it takes up the whole room?"
- Have students walk or run their individual paths. Make sure the students are careful not to run into one another. Traffic problems might be avoided if the class is divided into halves or thirds. It is fine if the students need the sheet of paper at first. Then encourage them to try it without the map.
- Ask the class if anyone sees someone performing the pattern that she or he drew. Be prepared for animated statements: "That's my pattern!" or "You didn't do the curvy part right!" or "That was supposed to be my pattern!"

Checking accuracy. If time allows, discuss how the dancing of these patterns might be done more accurately. How might lines on paper be accurately expanded into paths across a floor?
- One way to increase accuracy is to first draw an accurate map of the classroom on paper, then draw the path on the map, carefully noting how the path relates to landmarks in the classroom.
- Another way is to measure each segment of a drawn spatial pattern in inches. Then translate inches to another length. A fun conversion to use is: 1 inch = 1 body length. For example, if you started with an equilateral triangle with sides of five inches, you would have five students lay down on the floor end to end for each side of the triangle. Instead of using bodies to measure a floor pattern, what else could you use? A table? A chair? Have students create their own method for measuring.
- If the floor has a pattern on it, another way to do the conversion is to draw the path on grid paper, then convert each grid square on paper to one pattern unit on the floor.
- Ask students to think of other methods.

4-4. Path Dances (7-15 minutes)

In this exercise, several students perform the same path, but are free to locomote in different ways.
- Have the students get in groups of three or four. Each member of a group has a sheet of paper with a spatial path on it from the previous exercise (section 4-3), so each group has three or four spatial paths from which to choose.
- Have each group select one path for the group to learn. Each group should then practice moving along the same path at the same time, as in follow-the-leader.
- Have members of groups show each other their ways of locomoting.
- Using the one spatial path and the various ways of locomoting, have each group put together a dance. Students are free to locomote all in the same way, all in different ways, or in any combination. Similarly, they may start at different times or the same time.
- Have the groups demonstrate. Add music.

4-5. Altering Patterns (7-15 minutes)

In this activity students alter one aspect of a spatial path and perform that alteration clearly. This activity is a continuation of the previous one (section 4-4), so students remain in the same groups, and each group continues to work with the same spatial path.
- Have each member redraw the group's spatial pattern so one part of it is different in some way. Possible variations include:
  - Changing an angle or curve
  - Lengthening or shortening a section
  - Changing the scale and doing part of the pattern in a huge or very tiny way.

  If a group has a spatial pattern that is too complex, have them pick one of these simple spatial patterns.

- Have each member perform the variation for the other members of the group. Remind the students not to reveal what the variation is! Have the others in each group draw what they see. Now compare the drawings of the mover and the observers.
- Discuss the process.
- One group at a time, have everyone in a group simultaneously perform their new, personal paths. Encourage them to try to maintain the integrity of the paths, and to try not to bump into each other.
- Discuss how it looked. Ask students if the variations were clear. If not, discuss the difficulties in clearly performing the variations.

4-6. Extra Challenges

Here are some extra challenges for students who have just completed the previous section on variations in spatial paths. Remember that the spatial path is a point of departure for the creation of a dance; students do not have to stick exactly to the path if they do not want to, nor do they have to travel all the time.
- "Can you perform your pattern backwards?" "Can you reverse the orientation of your pattern (do the mirror image)?" "Can you do the sequence of movements in your pattern in the opposite order?" These three variations are all types of reversals. Can the students think of other interpretations of "reversal" which they can apply to the spatial paths?
- "Can you put two of your patterns together?"
- If the dance needs a beginning or ending, have students make one up. For example, ask students how the dancers get to their starting positions? Do they walk on stage? Do they rise up from the floor?
- Have students perform their variations to music. Or let music suggest the direction a dance should go.
- Have one student travel along a path, and at several points along the path, add gestures like raising the arms, turning, lowering the body to the floor, slowing down or speeding up. One by one, have all the students in a group imitate the first performer, entering the path when the previous performer reaches the first gesture point. This creates a canon in which all performers move through the same series of gestures, but at different times.
- Have students make a pattern that creates a loop by returning to its starting point (a figure eight is a simple example). Ask two students to start at different points on the loop and run around the path while staying the same distance away from each other. Try the same game with three or more students on the same path. This last assignment might also be valuable when choreographing a spatial path dance.
- If students are very clear about their paths, have two groups perform at the same time. Remind them to watch out, so they do not collide.

4-7. Reflection & Assessment

Critiquing the dance
Observe students carefully as they work and demonstrate. Here are some questions for gauging the progress of each student relative to their starting point.
- Did the clarity of the movement increase with practice?
- Did they students become more clear about using their centers when traveling? In other words, did they smooth out rough spots and gain control without loosing energy and size?
- Did they commit to creating and working on the dances? Did the dances take on their own character?
- Did the students perform or were they hesitant or afraid?

Clarifying the movement
Look for how the dancer's focus helps audience members see the spatial path more clearly.
- An adage among dancers is that walking is the hardest thing to do well. Paying attention to how the center moves will facilitate making changes in how the students walk. Notice whether the students move in such a way that their centers move in a straight line, up and down, or side-to-side. Particularly if the locomotor pattern does not move in a forward direction, or if it changes from forward to sideways to backward, clarifying how the center is moving will clarify the traveling and help to make it more efficient. Ask students to focus on their centers as they move.
- Transitions are a great place to make things more interesting. Are the transitions gradual or sudden? Sharp turns or transitions from one locomotor pattern to another cry out for creative solutions.
- Encourage students to notice how the focus of a performer helps the audience "see" the spatial pattern. What happens if the performer looks ahead at the next part of the path vs. looking off to the side? What happens if the performer seems to move purposefully versus wandering aimlessly?

Critiquing the mathematics
- Were students able to perform the spatial paths on the floor with some accuracy?
- Did they improve or correct their mistakes as they worked on the paths? What methods did they use to make corrections?
- "When you expanded your path to fill the room, what did you do in your imagination to help you decide where the path would go?" For instance, some students may have traced the path with their eyes, imagined drawing the path on the floor with a giant hand, imagined running along the path on the paper, or imagined superimposing the paper on the floor.
- In section 4-5 students create variations on paths. How can variations be accurately recorded? Is it better to record them all on one page, or on different pages? If on the same page, how are variations identified? By color, or some other means? How are they distinguished from the original spatial path?

Questions for discussion
Artists and scientists often deal with matters of scale.
- Make a list of sciences that study things that are very big. Make a list of sciences that study things that are very small. What sorts of models or maps does each science use? How do the scientists make sure the models are accurate?
- How far away would a stage have to be for a dancer to be the height of a baseball held at arms length?
- "Suppose you wanted to paint an exact copy of a drawing on paper so it fills a wall of a room. How could you make sure the copy looked exactly like the original, but bigger?" "Suppose you wanted to make a sculpture as large as you are that was an exact copy of a clay model that you could hold in your hand. How could you make sure the copy looked exactly like the original, but bigger?"
- "Architects make three-dimensional models of buildings. They also draw floor plans. Why do both?"
- "Suppose you wanted to make a miniature model of the neighborhood that includes your school. What scale do you think would be appropriate? One inch in your model would equal what distance in real life?" You can expand this question into a project by having the class draw a map or build a model of the school or local neighborhood. How do mapmakers measure and check accuracy?

- People who do special effects for movies often build small models that are filmed in such a way as to seem much larger than they are. For instance, the space ships in the first Star Wars movie (Episode 4: A New Hope) were models ranging in size from a few inches to a few feet across. Of course the effect is not always convincing. For instance boats on water in old science fiction movies often look fake. What gives the model away? One answer is that the water does not look right, even if you slow down the camera, because the way water sticks to itself is too "big" A clever solution to this problem is chemically modified "miniature water," which breaks up at a smaller scale.
- In the world of computer graphics programmers describe shapes by assigning each point on the surface of an object three numbers that are the x, y and z coordinates of the point. Multiplying every coordinate by a number other than 1 changes the scale of the object. What happens if you multiply by a number bigger than 1? What happens if you multiply by a number between −1 and 0? What happens if you add 5 to each x-coordinate?

4-8. Further Activities

Paths from art. Have students look at works of art (painting, sculpture, architecture, mosaic, poetry), and then derive spatial paths from them. For instance, in choosing locomotor patterns, let the colors, textures or language of the art works suggest ways of moving. Explore the question: Where else in the world might one find patterns and paths? Think of all the different things that move. Brainstorm.

Theme and variation. A major form that runs through many of the arts is called "Theme and Variation." For instance, composer Johannes Brahms wrote Variations on a Theme by Paganini for piano, and painter Claude Monet painted many series of studies which are essentially theme and variation, such as haystacks viewed at different times of day. Discuss with the class how theme and variation relates to this chapter. Where, in particular, are theme and variation found?

Morning path. Ask the students to draw a picture of the paths they followed to get from home to school this morning. "Simplify the shape of the path and walk it across the room. Perform a dance that tells the story of your journey from home to school as you move along the path."

4-9. Resources

Folk dances, particularly from Europe and the Middle East, often focus on group formations. (For example, line dances sometimes wind around and through themselves)

Modern dance and ballet choreographies are filled with inspired uses of spatial paths. Check out works by George Balanchine, Martha Graham, Laura Dean, Mark Morris, "Esplanade" by Paul Taylor.

The movie *The Agony and the Ecstasy*, based on the biographical novel by Irving Stone, includes the story of how Michelangelo painted the ceiling of the Sistine chapel. In making the movie the filmmakers had to research how Michelangelo transformed his drawings into a gigantic mural that covered a ceiling.

Franklin, Eric. *Dynamic Alignment Through Imagery.* Champaigne, IL: Human Kinetics, 1996. Using imagery to develop and improve alignment. Exercises that deal with initiating and carrying out movement.

Kluger-Bell, Barry, and the School in the Exploratorium. *The Exploratorium Guide to Scale and Structure: Activities for the Elementary Classroom.* Portsmouth, NH: Heinemann, 1995. "Body Balance," pp 97-99 has students explore with a partner the way bodies balance. The book compiles activities for the classroom that involve building and scaling.

CHAPTER 5
Threesies
An Introduction to Symmetry

Grades:	K-6
Time:	20-40 minutes
Topics:	Symmetry, visual thinking
Groups:	of 2 or 3
Space:	Requires clear floor
Materials:	Handout (page 51) for each student
	Pencil with eraser for each student
	(optional) Tape deck and music
Related Activities:	Chapters 6 *Watch Your p's and q's* and chapter 7 *Twisted Addition* develop symmetry further

This is an introduction to symmetry, with a focus on rotational symmetry. Although much of it is geared toward elementary-age students, it also works as a good introduction for older students (who might want to skip the hexagon-folding part of the lesson).

As we say in one of our shows, "It's much easier to *see* symmetry than to actually do it." Mirror, or reflection, symmetry feels natural because we have been trained by looking into mirrors: we raise our left hands, our reflections in the mirror raise their right hands. As you will discover, rotational symmetry is like looking into a bizarre mirror that refuses to reverse right and left, but with a bit of practice it can also start to feel natural.

Examples of rotational symmetry are everywhere (flowers, logos, games), and the study of symmetry serves as a wonderful bridge between the sciences and the arts: the same ideas that appear in geometry, biology, and chemistry also appear in architecture, art and dance. Moreover, rotational symmetry is a building block for other symmetries.

Math Dance with Dr. Schaffer and Mr. Stern • © 2001 Schaffer, Stern, Kim • www.mathdance.org

5-1. Facing A Partner (5-10 minutes)

Mirroring. This popular movement game is both an exercise in paying attention and in understanding symmetry.

- Ask students to work in pairs. Students stand a few feet apart, facing their partners. K-3 students might want to start sitting cross-legged rather than standing. The teacher might also demonstrate in the center with a student.
- Ask one person in each group to be the leader. The other person is the follower.
- "Leaders, make a simple shape. Followers, copy the shape as if looking into a mirror, so that you are the mirror image of your partner. For instance if the leader holds up the right hand, the follower holds up the left hand."
- "Leaders, start moving slowly and followers follow as if you are the mirror image. Move very slowly so your partner can follow. Take turns leading and following." After a while, ask students to switch who leads and who follows, so everyone gets a chance to play both roles.
- As students become more comfortable with the activity, suggest that students try the following "Move only your legs. Is following the legs more difficult than following the arms? Why or why not? Try pivoting a bit, or even turning all the way around. Does turning increase the difficulty? Why or why not? When following, where do you look or focus? You may find yourself using your peripheral vision."

Rotational Symmetry. Now try the same exercise with rotational symmetry instead of reflection symmetry.

- One person leads and the other follows, with both partners facing each other, but this time the follower does the exact same thing as the leader, as in the game Simon Says. For example, if the leader raises her right arm, the follower raises his right arm. If the leader leans to her left, the follower leans to his left.
- Take turns leading and following. Instead of imitating the leader in mirror image mode, the follower will lean in the opposite direction. Dancers have to do this often, and anyone can learn to do it.
- Many people find this more difficult than mirroring. Why might it be more difficult?

5-2. Folding the Hexagon (10-20 minutes)

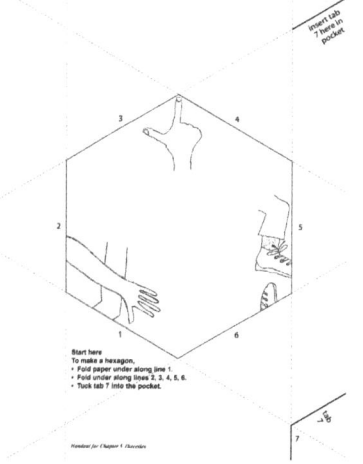

Fold the hexagon. Handout, one per student. (Note: older students may want to skip this section and continue on to Section 3)

- Hand each student a copy of the black-line master shown on page 51.
- Fold the paper down along the edges of the hexagon in the order listed. In other words, fold down along the line numbered "1" first, then "2," until all six sides are folded.
- Fold tab "7" down and insert into the slot. The final shape has six sides, and is called a hexagon.

Make the shapes on the hexagon.
- Have students get in groups of three. Have each group sit cross-legged in a circle.
- Ask the students to "Place your hexagons on the floor and move them together so the pointed fingers touch in the center and the hexagons fit together."
- "Now make that pointed-finger shape with your trio."
- "Do the same with the foot shape, and then the crossed arms shape."
- Can the trio make all three shapes on the hexagon *at the same time?*

> **Math note: 3-fold symmetry**
> The trios have just made shapes that have "3-fold" rotational symmetry. "Fold" means number of times in this context; thus the earlier rotational symmetry exercise involved "2-fold" or 180° symmetry. One way of thinking about rotational symmetry is that each person makes the exact same shape with the same orientation of limbs, but all facing toward the center of the circle.

5-3. Inventing Trio Shapes (5-15 minutes)

Make up new shapes. Using the hexagon as a guide, the students have made three shapes that have three-fold rotational symmetry.
- Now, using the whole body, each trio will invent 3 to 6 shapes that have three-fold rotational symmetry. (The younger the students, the fewer the shapes).
- Students may be standing up, lying down, upside-down, or in whatever position they like.
- Make sure that all three "petals of the flower" are the same. For instance, if one person crosses right arm over left, the other two must cross the same way. Or, another way to look at it is: If the group makes one complete revolution, their overall shape will coincide with itself three times. (Try this!)

Put the shapes in a sequence.
- Practice the shapes until the group can remember them exactly and know how to get into and out of the shapes without hesitation.
- Put the shapes in an order and learn how to move from one shape to the next.
- Practice the shape sequence until the group can move smoothly through all the shapes without talking or otherwise giving verbal cues.

5-4. Performing 3-fold Rotational Shapes (5-20 minutes, depending on class size)

- Go around the room and have each group perform their shapes.
- Each group may come to the center of the room to perform, or just stay where they are.
- If each group is assigned a number before starting, then the groups can perform all the trios one-at-a-time and uninterrupted.
- Try playing music while the trios perform. Music encourages students to treat this exercise more like a performance, and they may then pay more attention to how they move. See our suggestions for music at the end of the chapter *How to Use this Book*.
- If time allows, ask students if there is more than one way to get from one shape to the next. There are, of course, an endless number of ways to do this. Have the class make a list of possible transitions between shapes. Examples are fast or slow, moving in a circular motion or more directly, not remaining in rotational symmetry during the transition, and so on. Have students choose different approaches in their transitions. For example, if a group moves from shape 1 to shape 2 very slowly, then the next transition might be fast.

5-5. Hexagon Designs

Draw your shapes. Return to the paper hexagons. The paper has three shapes pre-drawn on it: a finger-pointing shape, a foot shape, and a arm-crossing shape, at three of the six corners.

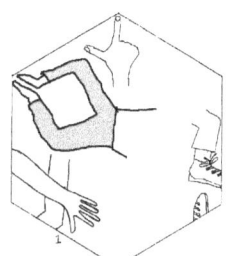

- Draw in the other three spaces of the hexagon the shapes that the group made up. This may be difficult, but it can be done.
- Try to line up the group's drawings the same way as at the beginning of this class. Do the shapes work?
- If they don't, erase them and try drawing them again. Save the hexagons.

Color the hexagons. You may want to save this activity for a separate session.

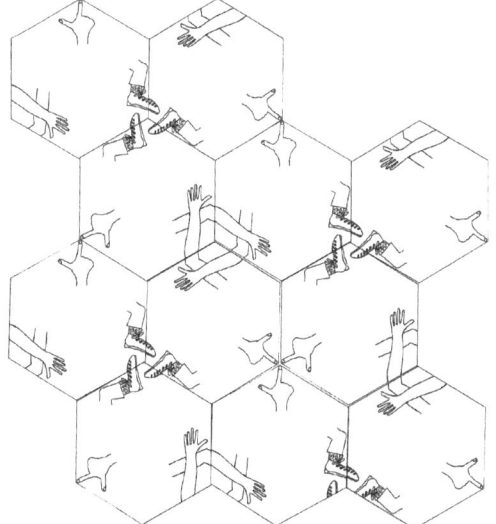

- Color the hexagons.
- When everyone has colored their hexagons, fit them all together on the floor. The resulting mosaic might have some enjoyable patterns.
- Look for points in the hexagon design where there is a three-fold rotational symmetry.
- Do you think the symmetry is broken if the colors are different? Why or why not?
- Decide as a group which areas should be colored in which ways and create another mosaic. Experiment.

5-6. Assessment and Reflection

Assessing the dance
- Did the clarity of the movement increase with practice?
- Did the dance phrase include the ideas we were working with?
- Did the students commit to creating and working on the dances?
- Did the students perform or were they hesitant or afraid?
- Were the transitions between shapes clear and quietly done (unless they decided to add sound as part of the dance)?

Assessing the mathematics
- For each particular exercise, were the symmetries correct?
- Was each dancer in a trio doing the same shape/movement?
- Were the students correctly distinguishing between reflection and rotation, and able to say which symmetries are present in various shapes or movements?

Questions for discussion
- This activity involved rotational symmetry in groups of three. Would it work for groups of 4 or 5 or 6? How about for groups of 20?
- Look through books with graphics or visual art and try to find the two types of symmetry we have been working with: mirror (sometimes called reflection) and rotation.
- How are mirror symmetry and rotational symmetry different? How are they similar?
- Can a shape have mirror symmetry *and* rotational symmetry at the same time? If yes, have the students make such a shape with their groups, or draw a picture of people illustrating it. If no, they should explain why not.
- In the pictures, were there any types of symmetry that are not one of these two kinds?
- List some ways to change a shape from symmetrical to asymmetrical.
- Because of the actual asymmetries between left and right in the human body, some movements may be difficult to execute in either reflection or rotational symmetry. For example, if the two partners are both right-handed, what actions might be difficult in reflection symmetry?
- What other asymmetries are found in the human body? Do they affect the difficulty of performing in symmetry?
- Which symmetry dances did the class like? Why? What makes the dances interesting?

5-7. Further Activities

Variations on the activities
- Vary the movement qualities and dynamics: sharp, slow, heavy, free-flowing, etc. A simple way to do this is to make a list of colorful adverbs, and try the same movements according to each.
- Change the type of music and see how that affects the performances.
- Change speed for different movements (for example: move into shapes 1, 3 and 5 quickly and into shapes 2, 4 and 6 slowly).
- Try making the transitions between shapes asymmetrical so they temporarily "break" the symmetry.
- Discuss as a group how to choose which variations to do. Try to do what would be best or most unusual or most enjoyable.
- Make one of the shapes asymmetrical, that is, not symmetrical. There are many ways to do this. See whether other groups can tell which it is.
- To go further, put all the groups in an order, create entrances and exits for each group, practice the sequence, and perform a rotational symmetry dance for other classes or the entire school.

Further research
- Find examples of circular symmetries in arts, culture and architecture.
- For example, find examples of logos which use circular symmetries.
- Find examples of public art or architecture which utilize circular patterns.
- Watch or learn square dances, and decide at what points any circular symmetries are present.
- In Scottish Country Dancing, it is considered normal to circle in a clockwise direction, as seen from above (called circling to the left); circling right is called "widdershins," which means "the witch's way." Find other examples of preferences in folk dance or world dance for one or the other direction in circular dances.
- Find objects around the house which use circular symmetries. Examples: kitchen implements, tools, electronic items. Decide which symmetries are present.
- When stuck in traffic, notice which symmetries are found on the hubcaps of nearby cars (they are surprisingly varied).

Square dance
Threesies focuses on rotational symmetry with groups of three people. With groups of four people we can explore more involved types of symmetry.
- Divide the class up into groups of 4 or 6. Have each play with improvisations that exhibit rotational symmetry. This is like doing the "Hokey-Pokey." The group arranges themselves around a central point and each person uses the same limb or movement, for instance "Put your left foot in and shake it all about," as in the song. A four person group might find themselves creating patterns found in square dances.
- Distinguish between those shapes which have rotational symmetry only and those that also have reflection planes. For example, when each person in the group faces the center while exhibiting bilateral symmetry (in which the right side of the body mirrors the left), the overall shape will also have reflection planes. How many planes?
- Have each group make shapes that exhibit only each of the following sets of symmetries:
    (a) Four-fold rotational symmetry and no others.
    (b) Four-fold rotational symmetry and four reflection planes.
    (c) Two-fold rotational symmetry and no reflection planes.
    (d) Two-fold rotational symmetry and two reflection planes.
- When the groups have learned how to differentiate between these symmetries, have them work more freely, inventing a series of shapes which they are able to cycle through smoothly without giving verbal cues. It is important to say, especially for non-dancers, that movement need not be dance class vocabulary. Ordinary movements work well here when performed with energy and clarity — and symmetry!
- Groups of 6 may also work on this exercise; they can look for 2-fold, 3-fold and 6-fold rotational symmetries, and 0, 1, 2, 3, or 6 reflection planes.

5-8. Resources

http://www.folkdancing.org/. Maintains a 120 page folk dance site, including a large U.S./Canada directory of folk dance groups and teachers.

Biedermann, Hans, translated by James Holbert. *Dictionary of Symbolism: Cultural Icons and the Meanings Behind Them.* New York: Meridian, 1989, translation 1992. several hundred symbols from world culture, many of them exhibiting circular symmetries.

Blackwell, William. *Geometry in Architecture*. Emoryville, CA: Key Curriculum Press, 1984. Elaborate tour of all the ways geometry appears in architecture. Profusely illustrated. By a professional architect with a life-long interest in geometry.

Carter, David E. *The New Big Book of Logos*. Headbone Interactive, 2000. A treasure trove of 2,500 logos, demonstrating many kinds of symmetries.

Chermayeff, Ivan, Tom Geismar, Steff Geissbuhler, and Geismar Inc. *Trademarks Designed by Chermayeff & Geismar*. Princeton, NJ: Princeton Architectural Press, 2000. Over 200 logos, showing many kinds of symmetries, by the outstanding design firm that created the NBC peacock, the Chase Bank octagon and the Alvin Ailey Dance human letterforms.

Dahlke, Rudiger. *Mandalas of the World: A Meditating and Painting Guide.* New York: Sterling Publishing Co., Inc., 1992. Over one hundred traditional mandalas, or circular designs, from around the world.

Herbison-Evans, Don. "Symmetry in Dance." Imprint, Technical Report 329, Basser Department of Computer Science, University of Sydney, Australia. (8 pages). Philosophical overview of symmetry in dance. (Lincoln Center Library, don@socs.uts.edu.au).

Reel, Rich. "FASR" and other Caller Terminology, 2001. http://www.all8.com/sd/calling/fasr.htm#symmetry. A detailed explanation, with diagrams, of symmetries in square dance. "FASR" stands for Formations, Arrangements, Sequences and Relationships. Part of "A Square Dance Caller's Notes" web site (http://www.all8.com/).

Zembrowski, Ernest Jr. *A History of the Circle.* New Brunswick, New Jersey: Rutgers University Press, 1999. The circle, its history and place in science and mathematics.

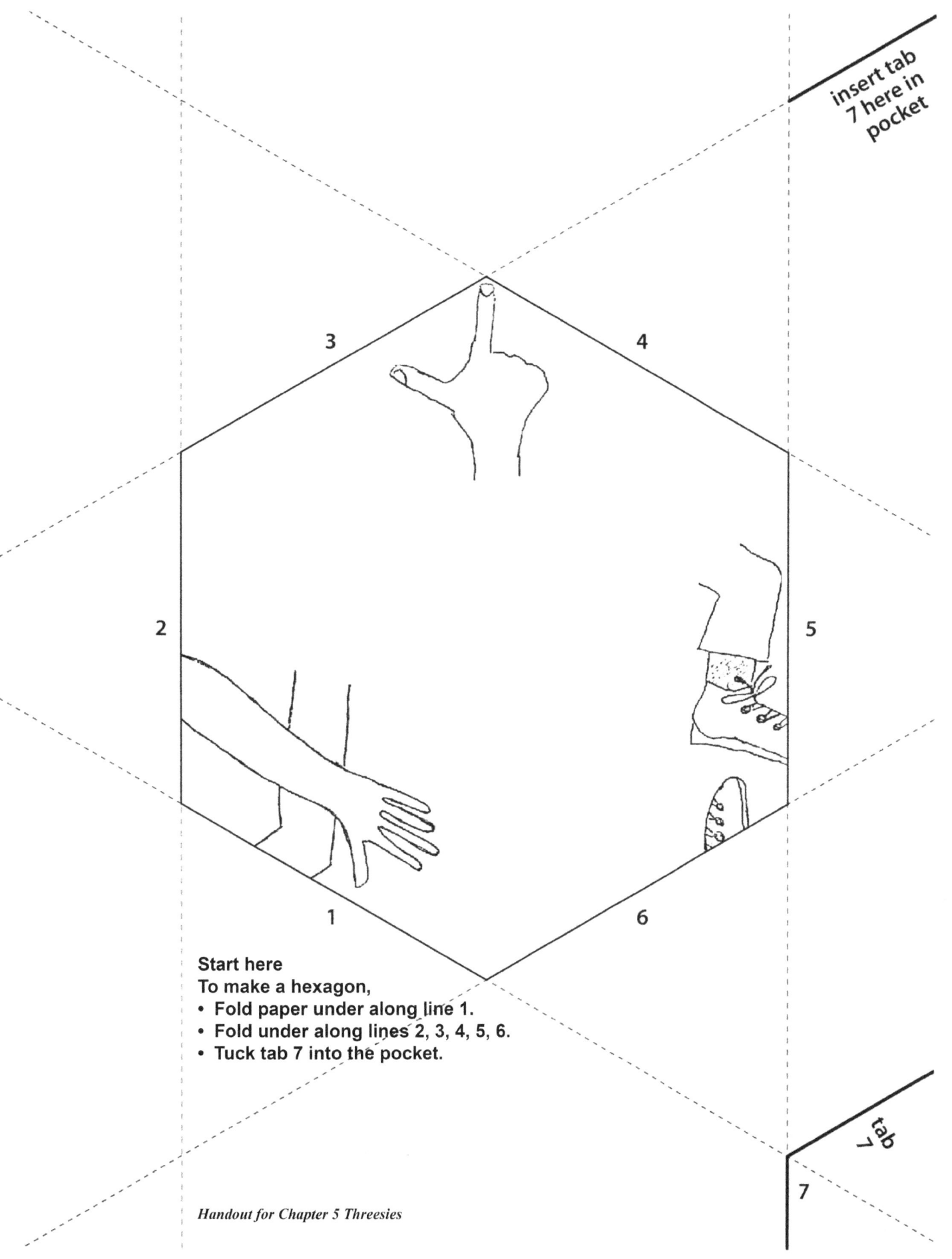

Start here
To make a hexagon,
- Fold paper under along line 1.
- Fold under along lines 2, 3, 4, 5, 6.
- Tuck tab 7 into the pocket.

Handout for Chapter 5 Threesies

CHAPTER 6
Watch Your p's and q's
Moving Through Four Types of Symmetries

Grades:	3-12
Time:	45 to 90 minutes
Groups:	duets, trios, quartets
Materials:	none
Space:	large, free of desks or chairs
Concepts:	math: symmetry, translation, rotation, reflection, glide;
	dance: repetition, opposition, reversal, inversion, regression, canon
Prerequisites:	Chapter 5 *Threesies*
Related Activities:	Chapter 7 *Twisted Addition* (follow-on)

Although most people seem perfectly capable of spotting the plentiful use of symmetry and pattern in dance and the arts, it is also common for the many types of symmetry to be lumped together into one basket. We have all seen what happens when a speaker giving a presentation puts a slide or transparency in the wrong way. If someone shouts "turn the slide around," or "reverse it," the speaker will often do something different than what we expected, and try flipping the slide around several times before getting it right. Part of the problem is that we lack words for describing symmetry operations accurately.

In this chapter we will carefully practice distinguishing and moving through four basic types of symmetries. The activities use a variety of movements from the wave of a hand to full-body motion. Most activities are suitable for a wide range of ages and movement skill levels. Although trained dancers might strive to perform the mirroring improvisations with great precision and beauty, the same activities also look striking when done by untrained movers or by children. Younger children may lack the physical concentration to do the more involved group work, such as "flocking" in section 6-3.

To help us remember the four types symmetries, and as a kind of shorthand, we will use the four letters p, q, b, and d. Notice that these four letters are all the same shape, but flipped around in different orientations. For example, if we look at p and q in the diagram below, we see that they are standing in mirror symmetry. If you imagine the letters as people seen from above, then p has its right arm raised, and q has its left arm raised.

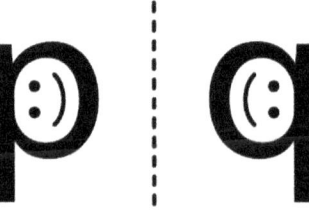

6-1. Do It on the Other Side (5-10 minutes)

In chapter 5, *Threesies*, we practiced making shapes in mirror or reflection symmetry as a warm-up exercise. We will do this again, but this time the way dancers tend to do it. Dancers often call the reversal of a movement in mirror symmetry "doing it on the other side."
- Ask the class to stand up and face front, with desks and tables cleared away
- Make a simple movement with one arm, and then say, "Do this on the other side, as if you were looking into a mirror." Tell the class to wait until they have seen the movement, and then try. In

Threesies we had the leaders move slowly, so the followers could follow at the same time. Now demonstrate more quickly, and see if they can remember and reconstruct it "on the other side."
- Repeat with another movement, gradually making them more difficult to follow. For example, slightly bring one arm in front of the other. Or step out forwards or backwards out of the plane facing the class. Or twist a little to the right or left. You may have to repeat each movement several times for the class to pick it up and reverse it.
- If you want to make the movement even harder to copy, try combining two or more of these "complicators:" Twist while stepping forward, or swing one arm in front of the other while leaning toward one diagonal.
- Try making up a slightly longer sequence of movements or gestures.
- Keep the movements simple — even small gestures provide substantial challenge.

6-2. What is Symmetry? (3-5 minutes)

"Symmetry" means two parts of an overall shape have the "same measure," just as "sympathy" means having the "same feeling" as someone else. Most definitions of symmetry refer to the ways in which a pattern repeats, is balanced, or is similar in shape to itself. We will not give a more formal definition of symmetry until a little later in this chapter, relying for the time being on the students' intuitive understandings of pattern.

This is a good time to have a preliminary discussion of symmetry.
- Ask the students what they think symmetry is.
- Make a list on the board of all the ideas and characteristics that they come up with.
- Ask them to point out occurrences of symmetry in the classroom.
- Incomplete ideas are also useful at this stage!

> **Dance and Math Note: Symmetry in the Arts and Sciences**
> The topic of symmetry is equally at home in dance and mathematics. Symmetry is found throughout dance, music, and the visual arts. Symmetry plays a key role in architecture, textile design and the decorative arts. It is also crucial in understanding wide areas of contemporary science from crystal structure to the intricacies of the quantum theory. Many of the breakthroughs in physics during the last century had to do with symmetry in the structure of space-time. Anthropologists use the symmetry in craft work to trace the history and influence of ancient civilizations.
>
> Symmetries in dance and music also include symmetries in time: one dancer or instrument repeats a phrase a certain number of beats after another. Or the phrase is repeated in the reverse order. The silent film comedian Charlie Chaplin was so adept at body movement that he sometimes acted scenes backwards, then ran the film backwards so the movement looked correct. This enabled him to safely perform stunts like having a car screech to a halt just in time to not hit him. It is extremely difficult to walk backwards so it looks normal when reversed in time.
>
> Other symmetries in dance include those derived from the similarity between the human body's silhouette as seen from the front and the back. Or choreography can make use of the resemblance in shape and motion between the arms and the legs, as in a cartwheel. More about symmetries in dance can be found in the Further Activities section 6-9.

6-3. Four Types of Symmetry (2-10 minutes)

Discovering types symmetries. This whole-class exercise lets students discover for themselves four of the basic types of symmetry. If you are short on time, skip directly to the section "Demonstrating types of symmetry."
- Have the class stand up and face the front.
- Face the class and raise one arm to make a pose. Ask students to make the same pose in one of four ways: they can choose to face front or face back, and they can choose to raise either their right or left arm. Ask students to face so they can see at least one other student.
- If you want to take this exercise further into movement, start slowly moving your body and ask students to copy you, or if a student cannot see you, to copy another student. Keep your movements slow and stay in one place. Twisting is okay, but more challenging, since some students may stop being able to see other students. This group movement is mesmerizing to watch!
- Return to a static pose. Now ask each student to look at another student and find words to describe how their two body positions are related. Remember that we are only interested in the relation between the two positions, not how each student is positioned. Write the words on the board. How many fundamentally different relationships are there? This question can lead to interesting discussion. Let students disagree; do not give the "correct" answer too early. It turns out that every pair of students is related by one of the four basic symmetries — translation, reflection, rotation or glide — though it is often tricky to see just how the symmetry applies.

Demonstrating types of symmetry. After acknowledging all the words students have found to describe symmetry relationships, introduce and demonstrate the four basic symmetry types. Ask all students to stand up.
- **Mirror**. Face toward the class, raise one arm (e.g. right), and ask students to raise the opposite arm (e.g. left). Move your arm and body slowly and ask students to imitate. Most students find this easy. This is called reflection or mirror symmetry.
- **Rotation**. Face toward the class, raise one arm (e.g. right), and ask students to raise the same arm (e.g. right). Move your arm and body slowly and ask students to imitate. Most students find this a bit trickier than mirror symmetry. This is called rotational or turning symmetry.
- **Translation**. Face away from the class, raise one arm, and ask students to raise the same arm. Move your arm and body slowly and ask students to imitate. Most students find this easy, though it can be tricky to coordinate since the leader and followers cannot both see each other. This is called translation or sliding symmetry.
- **Glide**. Face away from the class, raise one arm, and ask students to raise the opposite arm. Move your arm and body slowly and ask students to imitate. This is the most unusual of the four symmetries and can be tricky to master. This is called glide symmetry or glide reflection.

6-4. Translation or Sliding Symmetry (5-15 minutes)

The activities in the next four sections give students practice in distinguishing and embodying the four kinds of symmetries that appear when people stand in a row. If you do not have time to do them all in depth you can abbreviate the activities or leave out some of the symmetries.

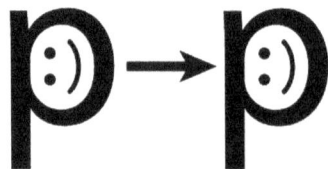

Let us start with translation. Notice that the two letters p in the diagram above are both raising their right arm; each may be moved to take the place of the other by sliding them along a horizontal line.

Students will work in groups of at least three for this series of activities. Moving slowly is essential here, because unlike the warm-up activity, students will move at the same time as the leader. Younger students might try these activities seated.

Following in translation symmetry

Follow the leader. Have students work in groups of three or four. This symmetry is present when two people make the same shape and face in the same direction. It is the kind of symmetry often seen in aerobics classes, where the teacher and students all face the front or the mirror. It is also seen in line dances in many traditional folk dance forms. (See section 6-10 Further Activities for clarification of this definition.)

- Each group chooses a leader. The other students face in the same direction as the leader, and attempt to duplicate the leader's movements.
- The leader begins by moving slowly, making simple movements with the arms. Add slow movements of the torso. Add slow and simple twists of the body.
- Here are some other types of movement to try. Do only as much as students feel comfortable with. Take one or two steps, being careful to "telegraph" the steps (that is, exaggerate the movements for preparing to take a step so other people can anticipate when you are about to take a step). If students seem to need more of a challenge, add gestures with the legs. Make steps to the front or back, then to the sides. Put two or more of the above together. For example, step to the side while twisting and raising the right arm.
- Change leaders and repeat.
- Ask each group to come up with a short movement phrase using this symmetry, and practice it till they can perform it without hesitation. Have each group demonstrate its phrase, and ask for brief comments and feedback from other students. A "movement phrase" is any short series of movements. For this exercise we recommend having each person choose a movement they saw someone else do that was interesting to imitate, then string those movements together to make a phrase.
- Critique the sense of ensemble in each group: were the students able to move together, as if they were one organism? What kinds of clues allow the leader to telegraph what will come next? Which types of movement were hardest to follow? As in the *Threesies* chapter, what attitudes, physical or mental, must one adopt to be able to follow and move with a group?

Flocking

Flocking. This is an intriguing and more challenging variation of follow the leader. Again, students work in groups of three or four.

- Begin by playing follow the leader. Now allow the leader to turn to face right; the group also turns in the same direction until a new leader is in front. That person now takes over the leadership role. Country and western line dances follow this pattern of having everyone move in unison, then turning everyone 90 degrees to face a new direction before repeating the dance. Flocks of birds also use this strategy, changing leader seamlessly when the flock changes direction.
- Continue doing this until everyone has had a chance to be leader. Try to develop the sense of ensemble to the point that it is not clear to an outside observer exactly who the leader is or when the switches are made. The trickiest part of flocking is the transition from one leader to another. See how smoothly the group can do this transition.
- Many flocks. If you have time, you can divide the class into several flocks of at least three people each. Allow two or more groups to work on the flocking (translation symmetry) exercise at the same time. Let the groups move around the room and pass through each other on occasion.
- Have the students discuss or write in their journals about their experiences.

Two flocks moving through each other

6-5. Reflection or Mirror Symmetry (5-15 minutes)

Notice that the letter p in the diagram is raising its right arm, while the letter q is raising its left arm; each may be reflected into the other about a vertical line between them.

This is the kind of symmetry you see when you look in the mirror. It is also common in dance classes: dance teachers often demonstrate the mirror image of the movement that the students are to do, and must learn the tricky task of saying things like," Raise your right arm like this," while actually raising the left! It also appears in a vaudevillian comedy sequence in the movie Duck Soup (performed by Harpo and Groucho Marx), and in the opening scene in the Patty Duke TV show, in which Patty Duke, playing herself and her own look-alike cousin, appeared to imitate each other as if a mirror were between them.

Remote Control. This exercise involves mirror image movement yet again, as in 6-1 *Do It on the Other Side*, but with a different emphasis.
- Have students work in pairs, standing up. One student is the leader, and the other is the follower.
- The leader moves slowly and the follower imitates in mirror image.
- The leader should try to get the follower to do things like sit in a chair, pick up an object, etc. Since objects in the room will be different for the two people, the leader might have to pantomime sitting in a chair while the follower actually sits in a chair.
- Can one person hand an object to the other person while moving in perfect reflective symmetry?

- Switch who leads and who follows from time to time.
- If there is enough time, groups can rehearse their movements and perform for the rest of the class.

Leader   Followers

Following in reflection symmetry

Mirror the Leader. Have students work in groups of three or four.
- Again choose a leader for each group. The leader faces the other members of the group. If the leader raises the right arm, the followers raise their left arms in mirror image form.
- Try to progress from arm motions, to movements of the torso, to a few steps through space, to twists outside the plane of the torso, to gestures with the legs and arms.
- Change leaders and repeat.
- Ask each group to come up with a short movement phrase, or adopt the same phrase that they invented in the translation section. Perform the phrase using mirror symmetry. The students may divide up so that there is not just one leader and several followers; for example four students might have two do the left side and two to the right.
- Have each group demonstrate its phrase, and ask for brief comments and feedback from other students. How did these differ from the look and feel of the translation phrases?

6-6. Rotational or Turning Symmetry (5-15 minutes)

Notice that the letter p in the diagram is raising its right arm, and the letter d to its right is also raising its right arm; each letter may be rotated 180° around the center point to take the place of the other. (Other rotational symmetries are explored in the chapter *Threesies*.)

One teacher told us this should be called "Simon Says Symmetry" because it is the kind of symmetry used in that game. It is observed when you see yourself in a video monitor in a store: you move your right arm and your TV image moves its right arm. It is the symmetry usually present when two people play "patty cake," and it is often seen in duets in the dance form Flamenco..

Near Miss. This exercise was inspired by the same comedic dance sequence that inspired chapter 1 *How Many Ways to Shake Hands?*
- Have students work in pairs, standing up. One student is the leader, and the other is the follower. Face each other, starting several feet apart.
- The leader walks slowly toward the follower and the follower imitates in rotational symmetry, being careful to step with the same foot as the leader.
- The leader should attempt to shake hands or otherwise greet the follower, but instead of shaking hands, miss each other so the two people never actually touch. Be sure to move slowly so the movements are not too hard to imitate.

- Explore different ways to circle around each other without touching, always staying in perfect rotational symmetry.
- Switch who leads and who follows from time to time.
- If there is enough time, groups can rehearse their movements and perform for the rest of the class.

Leader **Followers**
Following in rotational symmetry

Rotate the leader. Have students work in groups of three or four. One student is leader and the others are followers.
- This is more difficult to follow. The leader faces the followers.
- Again, the leader moves slowly, and makes more and more complex movements, as the followers attempt to follow in rotational or "Simon Says" symmetry. For instance, if the leader raises her right hand, then the followers also raise their right hands.
- Change leaders so that everyone in the group has a chance to lead.
- Again ask each group to come up with a short movement phrase using this symmetry, or adopt the phrase from the earlier exercises, and practice them.
- Have each group demonstrate its phrase, and ask for brief comments and feedback from other students. How did these phrases look in contrast to the earlier ones?

6-7. Glide Symmetry or Glide Reflection (5-15 minutes)

Glide is the symmetry of footsteps: each step faces the same direction as the previous step, but is reflected over the arrow line showing the direction of the feet to the other side. Of the four types of symmetry we have introduced, glide is by far the most difficult for people to recognize. Intuitively it might seem to be the combination of two operations — translation and reflection — although mathematicians consider it a single operation (and as we point out in the next chapter, every symmetry motion can be considered a combination of others.) As with the footsteps, the leader and the class face the same direction, but move in mirror image forms.

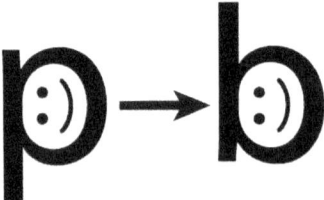

Notice that the letter p in the diagram is raising its right arm, while the letter q is raising its left arm; one may be turned into the other by sliding it along a horizontal line, then reflecting it about that same horizontal axis.

Ball pass. This trick exercise makes students think hard about glide symmetry.
- Have students work in pairs, standing up. One student is the leader, and the other is the follower. The leader starts facing in one direction, holding a hand-sized object like a book or ball in one hand. The follower stands directly behind the leader, facing the leader's back at arm's length.
- The leader takes a step slowly backward toward the follower and the follower imitates in glide symmetry, being careful to stay at a constant distance from the leader and always reverse left and right.
- The leader tries hand the object to the follower, which requires reaching back with one hand and forward with the other. This is especially tricky because the leader cannot see the follower. Then the leader tries to get the follower to hand the object back to the leader.
- Explore different ways to pass the object back and forth, always staying in perfect glide symmetry.
- Switch who leads and who follows from time to time.
- If there is enough time, groups can rehearse their movements and perform for the rest of the class.

Leader   Followers
Following in glide symmetry

Glide the leader. Have students work in groups of three or four. One student is leader and the other are followers.
- The leader faces away from the followers and begins to move slowly, first using arms, then torso, then small steps, then slight turns to right or left. The followers imitate in glide symmetry, being careful to reverse left and right.
- Change leaders and try again.
- Again ask each group to come up with a short movement phrase using this symmetry, or adopt the phrase from the earlier exercises, and practice them. Groups may wish to divide up those doing the left and right sides more evenly.
- Have each group demonstrate its phrase, and ask for brief comments and feedback from other students. How did these phrases look in contrast to the earlier ones?

6-8. Switching symmetries (5-15 minutes)

This advanced activity requires great sensitivity to different types of symmetry.

How can we move smoothly from one symmetry to another? It turns out that some positions exhibit more than one type of symmetry. From these positions of multiple symmetry a dancer can choose which symmetry to move into, as if stepping through a doorway between symmetries.

One simple doorway occurs when two dancers facing one another each reach both arms straight up. Their bodies exhibit both reflection and rotational symmetries, and so they can easily move into one or the other of these symmetries. When the lead dancer moves into an individually asymmetrical body position, such as with one arm up and the other down, the overall shape created by the two dancers will resolve into either mirror or rotational symmetry exclusively. There is a similar doorway between translation and glide symmetry. There are also doorways between reflection and translation, and between rotation and glide, but they require the dancers both face to the side, rather than in the same or opposite directions. Two of the symmetries have no doorways between them! (Which are they?) What kind of "doorway" facilitates moving between translation and glide symmetries? (See the chart on page 71 for a summary of these switches.)
- Have the students work in pairs, first taking turns improvising within each of the four symmetries introduced above, to make sure that they understand the differences between them. Remember that the

leader and follower face the same direction in translation and glide symmetry, and face in opposite directions (preferably towards each other) in reflection and rotational symmetry.
- Have the partners start moving in reflection symmetry, facing each other.
- When the leader's body reaches a position that is bilaterally symmetric, such as with both hands on the hips, the leader yells "switch". A person exhibits bilateral symmetry when the left and right sides of the body make the same shape, but in mirror image form. That means the person cannot be leaning or twisting to one side, but might be kneeling or arching backwards.
- Instead of imitating in reflection symmetry, the follower now imitates the leader in rotational symmetry. Continue moving until the leader reaches another bilaterally symmetric position and yells "switch." Keep alternating between reflection and rotational symmetry.
- Change leaders from time to time.
- Can the students become proficient enough to follow when the leader does not say "switch?"

When two people both exhibit bilateral symmetry, they can switch between translation and glide symmetry.

- Do the same switching between translation and glide symmetries. This time partners start facing the same direction. Start moving in translation symmetry, and when the leader reaches a bilaterally symmetric body position, the leader yells switch and the follower now imitates in glide symmetry. Again, change leaders from time to time. A good way to change leaders is to simply turn around so the leader faces the follower, and the two people change roles so the follower becomes the leader.

6-9. Reflection and Assessment

Assessment. Because symmetry spans mathematics and dance, we will not list dance and math assessment questions separately here. Students should be assessed in the following four areas:
- **Identifying and naming** the symmetries. The key idea is that there is more than one kind of symmetry, and that we can learn to distinguish among the various forms. Do students use the correct vocabulary when describing different symmetries? (We find that students often like to make up their own names for some of the symmetries, for example, Simon Says instead of rotation, and Aerobics instead of translation. This is a healthy way for them to gain power over the concepts, as long as they realize their terminology is not standard!) Students may be questioned individually to see whether they can correctly name the symmetries present in a movement or visual pattern. Simple visual designs allow for written tests. For example, the letters p, q, d, and b, exhibit symmetries of one another in many typefaces. Which symmetry is present here: "d q"? What other symmetries can be found in the alphabet?
- **Creating and performing** symmetric patterns. Are students able to use the four types of symmetries accurately and imaginatively in the various small group movement exercises? Ask students, working in groups, to make a short movement phrase which exhibits each of the four kinds of symmetries studied in this section. Did they actually use all four, and can they correctly say when the transitions between the symmetries occurred? Ask them to write a short paragraph detailing the differences and similarities between reflection and glide symmetries.
- **Critiquing** the use of symmetry in performance. Can students correctly name the symmetries they see in performances and critique their use? Students might critique other groups in class, or videos of dance or gymnastic performances. How exactly was the symmetry executed? What movements or shapes made particularly good use of the symmetry? How did the symmetry support (or detract from) the overall intent of the dance or gymnastics routine?

- **Making connections.** Can students relate the symmetries in the movement exercises to symmetries in other art forms and disciplines?

Discussion questions
- Discuss the difficulty or ease of performing translation, reflection, rotation, and glide symmetries. Which are easy, and why is that the case?
- Which are difficult? Why?
- Make lists of some of the things that help you distinguish these four symmetries. (For example, in translation and glide the leader and the followers face in the same direction, while in reflection and rotation they face in opposite directions.)
- What happens if the leader turns more than 90° to the right or the left? What happens if the leader turns completely around?
- What happens in reflection or rotation symmetries if the students are facing away from each other? (Do they need to look over their shoulders, for example, to see what the leader is doing?)
- Have the students write their own definitions of these four symmetries in their journals or to hand in. They may wish to draw little diagrams of people, or utilize the letters p, q, d, and b.

6-10. Further Activities

Dance

Perform the symmetries. Have the students create a series of movements, mostly exhibiting the symmetries we have been working with, and practice them so that they can show the class. We say "mostly" showing symmetry because sometimes the breaks from symmetry can be refreshing and interesting. Have the students vary the rhythm, size, and dynamics of their movements within their choreography.

Use music. Try playing recordings of various types of music while the students perform their movements. Beautiful patterns are easily created and can give students the understanding of what it takes to produce a dance phrase. Again, it is important to stress that non-dance vocabulary is wonderful — perhaps even preferable — everyday movement can take on beautiful qualities when performed in unison and with clarity and commitment. Examine the symmetries found in the music, as well as using it to accompany the movement.

What symmetry does this figure show?

A puzzle with the hands. Grasp the fingers of your left hand with those of your right, with the right thumb pointing up and the left thumb pointing down. Does this shape have one of the types of symmetry we have been discussing? Can you think of other examples of this kind of symmetry? This three-dimensional symmetry is sometimes called point-reflection (or point-inversion, rotary reflection, or even rotary inversion). It is as if there is a point centered between the two hands, and one hand is carried through the point, much as the light rays through a camera's aperture, to form the other hand.

Do the Opposite. Here is a further, more open-ended exercise that gets the class thinking about symmetry a little more divergently. It might be interesting to compare the responses from classes who have and have not been introduced to the four symmetries practiced in this chapter.

- Facing the class, wave your right hand: start the wave at shoulder height and reach upwards as you wave. Then say, "Do the opposite." You might get a variety of responses. For example, one person might wave the left hand, another person might wave a leg, and yet someone else might shake a fist.
- Make a note of the responses on the board. Notice that asking for the opposite action seems to be a more open-ended question than asking for the same action.
- Now do something very different from waving your hand: for example, write a note on a pad of paper. Then say, "Do the opposite of this in the same way that you did the opposite of the wave." Again note the responses.
- Choose one of the responses and say, "Now do the opposite of that." Continue building a sequence of opposites by choosing one of the class responses each time.

Other symmetries in dance.
- Have the students work in pairs experimenting with other sorts of symmetries, such as reversal (exchanging front and back), retrograde (performing movements backward in time), and inversion (reversing the order of a series of movements, but not the individual movements).
- Find movements or movement sequences which are difficult or impossible to reverse, retrograde, or invert. Why will they not work?
- Add these elements to the movement studies created earlier.
- Ask the students to be clear about which symmetries they are using.
- See whether the class can correctly pick out these symmetries.
- How is the dance phrase affected by each of these symmetries?
- View videotapes of contemporary dances and discuss the uses of symmetry in the choreography.

Dance Note: Symmetries in Dance

There are many more kinds of symmetry than we have explored here, for example, the symmetries between arms and legs, or symmetries in time.

Canon. Translations in time, in dance and music, are often known as **canon**. One dancer performs a movement phrase, and a short time later a second performs the same movements, with the same left/right orientation, and perhaps the same facing. Choreographers often play with these conventions, sometimes having the second perform in a different direction, or "on the other side." A third dancer might do the same phrase to extend the canon. When one dancer performs the same phrase repeatedly, the term **repetition** is often used. However, as with the common use of the word symmetry, its definition is also quite broad.
- Which exercise(s) in this chapter involved the use of canon?
- Have the groups add the element of canon to the movement phrases they developed earlier in the chapter.

Opposition. This is the relationship between arms and legs that is seen when most people walk normally: the left arm swings forward as the right leg steps, and vice versa. The mathematical term sometimes used for this is **screw displacement** (or screw rotation). It is as if the legs were spiraled upwards around the spine to take the place of the arms.
- An amusing exercise is to ask people to walk while concentrating on making sure that their arms move in opposition to their legs; for some reason thinking about this often makes it harder to do! (Then ask them to walk so that they do not use opposition!)

The word opposition is sometimes also be used to denote a shape in which the arms may be rotated to take the place of the legs and vice versa. This is often seen in ballet positions; in this picture imagine the dancer's body rotated 180° about the line shown, so that the arms and legs take each other's place. Choreographers may use symmetries — or harmonies — such as this between arms and legs to support the artistic statement of the dance.

Reversal. In addition to the strong bilateral symmetry in the human body, there is an approximate symmetry between the front of the body and the back, expressed as a mirror reflection through the "frontal" plane shown here:

This is made apparent when we see someone in silhouette — it is difficult to figure out whether the person is facing towards us or away from us. The dancer and choreographer Merce Cunningham developed a dance technique which challenges the dancer to reverse movements through this plane. Thus the reversal of an extension of the right leg forward would be a similar extension to the back. Some movements are difficult to reverse in this way, for example, many movements of the arms. For this reason Cunningham Technique often reverses a right arm movement to the front, for example, by changing it to the same movement of the left arm to the front.

Retrograde. The movement is performed as if time were reversed. Thus a leap forward from the left leg to the right leg is retrograded to become a leap backward from the right leg to the left! Needless to say, many movements are quite difficult to retrograde.

Inversion. A sequence of movements is inverted by performing them in the reverse order. So a hop on the left leg followed by wave of the right arm inverted becomes a wave of the right arm followed by a hop on the left. Some sequences cannot be inverted without changing transitions between movements considerably.

The terms reversal, retrograde, and inversion do not have standard definitions among dancers. Those we have given were used frequently by postmodern choreographers of the 1960's and 70's to play with audience expectations about the ways that movement was habitually organized. For example, one choreographer created a dance in which the performers had to respond immediately to the director's improvised commands to invert or retrograde the section of the dance they were performing at that moment.

Notice body symmetries. Notice the symmetries around you everyday. Find each of the symmetries we have described, and make notes about what you or the people you were watching were doing when you observed these symmetries. In addition to looking for symmetry as they walk down the street, students might look for them in sports activities, public areas, television, or the classroom.

Visual Arts. Explore the symmetries in the work of artists, for example M.C. Escher. Escher studied the symmetries found in Islamic art and applied them to his own work. Read about the Alhambra, the Islamic temple in Spain that Escher visited in his studies of tessellations (repeating patterns in the plane in which the shapes leave no gaps and do not overlap). Examine the symmetries found in public art, or in the craft work from various cultures. Create artistic designs utilizing symmetry.

Literature. Examine symmetry in language as well as in visual arts. Poetry often uses repeating rhythmic structure. Palindromes such as "A man, a plan, a canal, Panama!" by Leigh Mercer, read the same backward and forward. (See the references for this chapter.) How else can one find or create symmetries with words? Look up the symmetric letter form play of Scott Kim at www.scottkim.com, and invent some "inversions."

Other symmetries in mathematics and science. Investigate the literature on symmetry (see references). For example, there are more than four types of symmetry transformations if we do not restrict ourselves to the plane. Martin Gardner's *The New Ambidextrous Universe* discusses symmetry in biology, chemistry, and physics, as well as in mathematics and the arts. Here are some question he poses:
- A mirror reverses right and left, why doesn't it reverse up and down?
- What kind of mirror would not reverse right and left?
- What kind of mirror would reverse up and down?

Hop, skip, and jump. If we restrict ourselves to applying the four symmetry transformations in this chapter to patterns in a straight line, then there are actually seven ways they combine to give symmetric linear patterns, called frieze patterns. The mathematician John Conway came up with a set of descriptions using footprints and steps called the "hop-skip-jump" terminology:

p	pq	bd bd bd bd	p	d	pq	bd bd bd bd
p	pq		q	p	bd	
p	pq		p	d	pq	
p	pq		q	p	db	
hop	jump	sidle	step	spinning hop	spinning jump	spinning sidle

- Try to do each of these movements. The letters p and d represent the left foot (forward and backward facing), while q and b represent the right foot (forward and backward facing).
- Decide which of the four symmetries that we studied are found in each of these seven patterns.
- Form a line of people and have them move together using each of these patterns.
- Read more about this in Chapter 5.3 of *Symmetry, Shape, and Space*, by Kinsey and Moore.

Math Note: the Mathematical Definition of Symmetry

In the interest of sketching out the larger ideas quickly, we have been a shade inexact with out mathematical definitions in this chapter. And mathematics can be as exacting as... the steps of classical ballet! We have introduced four types of symmetry: translation, reflection, rotation, and glide. A more precise statement would be that these are four possible "rigid motions" or "isometries" in the plan or along a line, that is they are transformations which move an object without changing its size or shape.

Symmetry is present when we have a group of dancers whose overall shape is not changed by one of these rigid motions. For example, if four square-dancers standing in a circle move one quarter turn clockwise, then they will end up making the same shape in space as when they began, each person taking the place of the person to their left. Although the people have changed places, the overall group shape remains the same.

However two dancers in a line, such that one is the translation forward of the other, do not exhibit translation symmetry unless the line of dancers extends indefinitely in both directions! (Why?) Clearly this is impossible, even in the long lines at the Department of Motor Vehicles. But choreographers often use a trick to suggest this image: a line of dancers performing the same movements emerges from offstage left and proceeds across the stage to exit on the right:

Glide symmetry similarly requires a line of dancers extending in both directions, rather than just two dancers. We hope we have erred on the side of clarity!

6-11. Resources

Donner, Michael. *I Love Me, Vol. 1: S. Wordrow's Palindrome Encyclopedia.* An encyclopedic investigation and listing of palindromes.

Gardner, Martin. *The New Ambidextrous Universe: Symmetry and Asymmetry from Mirror Reflections to Superstrings.* New York: W. H. Freeman and Company, 1990 (3rd revised edition of work originally published in 1964). A beautifully written and engaging survey of symmetry and asymmetry.

Hofstadter, Douglas. *Godel, Escher, Bach: An Eternal Golden Braid,* New York: Basic books, 1979 20th Anniversary Edition 1999. *Metamagical Themas: Questing for the Essence of Mind and Pattern.* New York: Bantam Books, 1985, and *Fluid Concepts and Creative Analogies: Computer Models of the Fundamental Mechanisms of Thought.* New York: Basic Books, 1995. Hofstadter is obsessed with the symmetries in art, literature, and science, and has created wonderful and playful studies. See his chapter on self-reference in *Questing*; also his game Tabletop in *Fluid Concepts* in which two people try to imitate each other's actions.

Kim, Scott. *Inversions: a Catalog of Calligraphic Cartwheels.* Berkeley, CA: Key Curriculum Press, 1996 (originally published in 1981). Playful and humorous artwork using symmetry and letterforms, with a guide to creating inversions of your own.

Kinsey, L. Christine Kinsey, and Teresa E. Moore. *Symmetry, Shape, and Space: An Introduction to Mathematics Through Geometry.* Emeryville, CA: Key College Publishing, 2002. A very readable and accessible introduction to symmetry and geometry, designed for non-science majors. See chapter 5.3 on Conway's hop, skip, and jump frieze patterns.

Langdon, John. *Wordplay: Ambigrams and Reflections on the Art of Ambigrams.* New York: Harcourt Brace Jovanovich, Publishers, 1992. Playful symmetric constructions with letterforms.

O'Daffer, Phares G. and Stanley R. Clemens. *Geometry: An Investigative Approach*, and *Laboratory Investigations in Geometry.* Addison-Wesley, 1976. A text for prospective teachers which includes many activities dealing with symmetry.

Stevens, Peter S. *Handbook of Regular Patterns: An Introduction to Symmetry in Two Dimensions.* MIT Press, 1992. Voluminous compendium of visual patterns in design, ornament, quilting and crafts from all over the world.

Wechsler, Robert A. *Analysis of 'Reversals' in the Cunningham Dance Technizue. Issues Concerning the Perception of Symmetry in Dance,,* in Lincoln Center Library collection. Contact: robert@palindrome.de

Weyl, Hermann. S*ymmetry.* Princeton Univ. Press, 1952. A classic illustrated introduction to symmetry.

CHAPTER 7
Twisted Addition
Combining one symmetry with another

Grades:	4-12
Time:	1 hour
Groups of:	1-4
Materials:	handout
Space:	large, relatively free of desks or chairs
Concepts:	Dance: movement combinations
	Math: symmetry, pattern, angle, modular arithmetic, complex numbers
Prerequisites:	Chapter 5: *Threesies*, Chapter 6: *Watch Your p's and q's*

Reflection + Reflection = Translation

In Chapter 5, *Threesies* and *6, Watch Your p's and q's*, we introduced mathematical symmetries that appear in motions along a line or in a circle, as well as several symmetries in time. In this section we show how combining (or "adding") symmetries leads to new patterns. The mathematical ideas underlie what is known as the theory of symmetry groups, and the activities show how algebraic structure can be glimpsed in how we move around the world everyday. They are also key concepts in contemporary sciences such as crystallography, quantum theory, and chemistry.

We first played with these ideas in a dance entitled *Lost in Translation,* in which three characters talk about and act out concepts of symmetry, all the while getting more and more mixed up. Watching performers get confused by complex operations can be fun for the audience! Other contemporary choreographers have also enjoyed playing games with symmetries in time and space; sometimes the games are made visible to the audience, sometimes they are known only to the performers who must master them.

In the performing arts images are often fleeting, and symmetries may be difficult to analyze. In the visual arts, however, the work may be examined at length, so we can often more easily glimpse the richness of symmetry. In all the arts symmetry and asymmetry are important elements of composition, and in this chapter we hope to make more apparent how they work.

7-1. Symmetry Improvisation (5-10 minutes)

This improvisatory movement game gets students interested in how symmetries combine. It is quite interesting to watch.
- Have students work in small groups of 3 or 4.
- Ask one student in each group to start repeating a brief gentle movement, such as slowly waving an arm, twisting in one direction then the other, or stepping forward then back. The movement should be brief, about two seconds long, and stay rooted in one place. Remind students to repeat the movement clearly and accurately; changes in the movements, or unintended extraneous moves make the repeating movement more difficult to imitate. In addition to being a study in symmetry, this is a great way to get students to be clear about communicating movement with their bodies.
- A second student joins in, copying the movement of the first student. The second student can choose the same movement as the first student, or the mirror image of the movement, and can stand anywhere near the first student, pointing in any direction. Of course it is best if the second student [where is the rest of the sentence?]
- A third student joins the first two people, again copying the movement, choosing where and in what direction to do the movement. Repeat until all members of the group are moving.
- Then the first student moves to a new position and continues copying the movement. The second student moves to a new position and copies the movement, and so on.
- Explore the different effects that different spatial relations create. For instance, what happens if everyone points in the same direction? What sort of feeling does direct imitation create as compared with mirror image imitation?

7-2. Spinning Doll (10-15 minutes)

As the doll turns. This warm-up exercise will get the students visualizing and trying out combinations of symmetry motions. They will begin to break down and analyze movement mathematically.
- Hold a doll up facing the class. Show what happens when it does a half-spin: it ends up facing away from the class, but right side up.
- Again face the doll right side up toward the class, and show the result of a half-cartwheel: the doll ends upside down, but facing the class.
- Finally, return the doll to the right side up toward the audience position, and show the result of a half-somersault: the doll ends upside down, but facing away from the class.

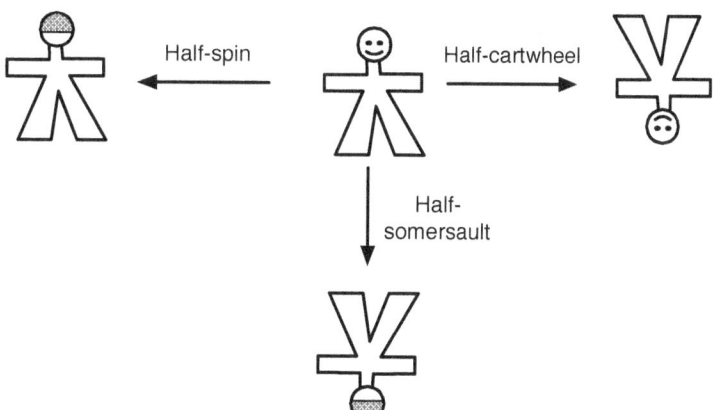

Imagining the result of several turns. Ask the class to discuss the following question in groups of three or four: if the doll starts right side up and facing the class, and then does a half-cartwheel, followed by a half-spin, followed by a half-somersault, which way will it end up facing?

- The class should first try to imagine the motion of the doll, without using an object to help.
- Then, if necessary, they may use their hands to mimic the motion of the doll.
- If anyone is really energetic — or if the class is comfortable with heavy physical activity, for example a physical education class or a gymnastics class, then this activity may be done with bodies rather than a doll. In this case the students will need to work in pairs, and be able to support each other doing handstands. Since this may be unsafe for non-trained movers, an alternative is to have one student act out the movements while lying on one side of the body:

Changing the order of turns. After students have successfully answered this question, ask them to put these three movements into a different order. (It may help to have the class list all possible orders on the board – they should come up with a total of six.) Does the doll also end up facing the same way after, for example, a half-spin, half-cartwheel, and then half-somersault?
- Compare notes — did all groups find that order does not matter, and that the doll always ends up facing the way it started, no matter what order the three motions are done? (Note: When you add up numbers the order does not matter, but when you add three-dimensional rotations, surprisingly, the order usually does matter. However in the case of adding half-turns it makes no difference.)
- If they are the same, can anyone think of an explanation why this must be the case? (Note: think about how the half-somersault and the half-cartwheel reverse top and bottom, and how the half-somersault and the half-spin reverse front and back.)
- Can anyone think of other examples where three halves "make a whole?"

7-3. Combining Symmetries in a Line (20-30 minutes)

Review the four kinds of mathematical symmetry motions we studied in chapter 6 *Watch Your p's and q's*: translation, reflection, rotation, and glide. What happens when two of these symmetry operations are done one after the other? Ask for three volunteers to come up to the front of the class and model the following situation:
- A stands behind B
- B raises one arm and A follows in glide symmetry.
- Then C stands in line with A and B in 180 degree rotational symmetry with respect to B.
- Next B steps out of the way, leaving A and C in which symmetry? Answer: The combination of glide (A and B) followed by rotation (B and C) yields a reflection (between A and C).
- If the students seem comfortable with these symmetries, have them move slowly and continuously in these symmetries, with B following A, and C following B. The other students will then see the symmetries in motion, rather than in static positions.

A and B in glide symmetry   *B and C in rotational symmetry*   *A and C in mirror symmetry*

Fill in the chart. Our goal is to try all combinations of two symmetries and make a table showing the results. You may need to have your volunteers model one or two more such combinations to help the class understand how to do this. Draw the chart below on the board in front of the class. Notice that:
- The first symmetry between A and B is represented by the left hand column.

- The second symmetry, between B and C is represented by the top row.
- The result is written in the chart in the corresponding row and column.

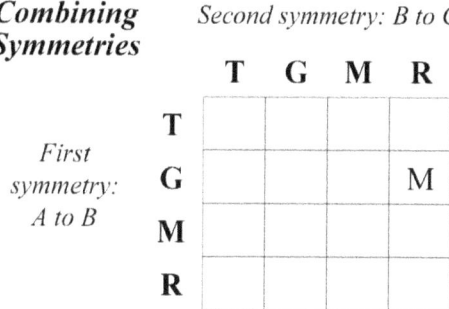

Notice also that we have used T for translation, G for glide, M for mirror or reflection, and R for rotation.
- Divide the class into groups of four, have them choose an unfilled in space in the chart, model the symmetry combination, and then report back on how to fill in that space. Make sure they actually act out the symmetry, rather than make a guess based on the patterns in the chart as it fills up!
- The class may need a few more demonstrations of the process before they understand it. Monitor their work; if they make a mistake have them go back and try again.
- Or give every group a copy of the handout on page 76 and have them fill in the entire chart on their own. It is even more important in this case to walk around and monitor their work.
- The completed chart should look like this:

Combining Symmetries

Second symmetry: B to C

First symmetry: A to B

	T	G	M	R
T	T	G	M	R
G	G	T	R	M
M	M	R	T	G
R	R	M	G	T

Find patterns
- Once the chart has been filled in correctly on the board, have the students make a list of all the patterns that they see in the chart.
- They will probably notice many symmetries within the chart itself. For example, there is a reflection symmetry through each of the two main diagonals, and 180° rotational symmetry about the center. Also each letter appears once in each row and column.
- Can the students explain why any of the patterns they have found must be there?

Math Note: Group Theory

The subject of how to combine symmetries is known in mathematics as group theory, and it appears in many areas of mathematics and physics. Students are often amazed that the combination of two symmetry motions always yield a third. They are seeing an algebraic system that encapsulates how we move our bodies around in space. This is not the algebra of numbers that they may be used to, but like any algebraic system, it uses symbols to encode more complex ideas, and includes a set of rules and patterns for how to combine the symbols. The whole idea of adding things other than numbers is the basis of abstract algebras — a major area of modern mathematics. Dance notation is another form of algebraic system. All such systems obtain power from the fact that some patterns may be more easily discerned once the thing they encode, in this case movement, is translated into this succinct form.

7-4. Symmetry Dance (15 minutes)

Improvising with multiple symmetries. This improvisatory exercise is the basis for the next compositional exercise.
- Have the students work in groups of three.
- One student is the leader. A second student chooses a symmetry (translation, reflection, rotation or glide) with which to follow the movements of the leader. The third student chooses a symmetry with which to follow the movements of the second.
- The leader moves slowly, and the followers follow. For instance the leader might raise an arm, step out with one leg, or twist from the waist. What happens when someone turns a little too far to the side?
- Take turns being leader, and try different movements and symmetry combinations.

Dance note: Composing a movement phrase

In the following activity, as well as many others, we ask students to compose a movement phrase, which is any series of movements that we can then treat as a unit of a larger performance. Although the authors' orientation towards dance allows any type of movement, we can still offer some guidelines for what makes a good movement phrase and how to create one.

A movement phrase is like a sentence in speech. Phrases vary in length from a few seconds to a few minutes in length. For our purposes in this book phrases should be kept short, about five to ten seconds long. A good phrase should involve clear movements that are easy to repeat or teach another person. Avoid movements that are tentative or too small. Try to make a phrase that has a clear beginning and end, with a sense of progression in between.

We realize that a blank canvas can be intimidating. How can one choose when everything is permitted? A good way to get started is to ask each person in a small group to invent a single movement, then string the movements together to make a phrase. Once students have something to work with they will more easily find ideas about what works, what doesn't, and how to improve it.

Students do not have to plan the whole phrase at once. They might try something, then ask themselves what comes next. Remind them that they can always change a phrase if they do not like it. Tell them to give themselves permission to experiment. Some of the best ideas are derived from failure.

The movements do not have to look like any particular style of dance. Simple everyday movement is fine. We encourage students to explore the full range of ways the body can move: move different parts of the body, twist or bend, expand or contract, change level (move the center of gravity up or down), shift where weight is supported, approach or move away from another dancer, or jump into the air.

Composing with multiple symmetries. This challenging dance composition exercise builds on the previous symmetry improvisation.
- Students continue working in their groups of three.
- Compose a short movement phrase for one person to do, by putting three distinct movements in sequence. You can choose movements that were interesting to imitate in the symmetry improvisation above, or invent new ones. See the dance note above for more ideas on making movement phrases.
- Learn to perform the phrase as a group, with everyone moving together, all facing the same direction. Practice the phrase until the group can perform it smoothly.
- Now learn this variation involving reflection symmetry. One student — the leader — performs the phrase normally. The second student copies the first student, but in mirror image. The third student copies the second student in mirror image. Student can be near or far from each other, facing in the same or different directions. Again, everyone moves together, not one after another.
- One student — the leader — performs the phrase normally. The second student copies the first student, but in 180° rotational symmetry. The third student copies the second student, again in rotational symmetry, but using a different center of rotation. Again, everyone moves together, and students can be near or far from each other.

- Work on developing a sense of ensemble, even when performers face different directions, or move in opposite directions. Practice the three symmetries until you can perform them without hesitation.
- Some groups may want to experiment with other symmetry combinations. For instance a group of four students could move all facing different directions. Or the group could split in half, with two people doing the same movement in translation while the other two imitate in glide.
- Choose an order in which to perform the three symmetries. You do not have to start with translation. Find ways to make transitions between phrases. Complete the composition by adding a beginning and ending. During beginning, transitions and ending the performers do not have to move symmetrically.
- Have the students take turns showing their work to the rest of the class. The class should discuss what they see. Students may find it challenging to correctly identify the symmetries used, and the places where transition occur between them. Observation and discussion are important ways for students to solidify their understanding.
- Have the students do more work on their phrases. They may wish to discuss how they feel about the phrases created, and what images or ideas they bring to mind, before creating a beginning and an ending that are in concordance with those feelings.
- Try playing recordings of various types of music while the students perform their movements. Beautiful patterns are easily created and can give students the understanding of what it takes to produce a dance phrase. Again, it is important to stress that non-dance vocabulary is wonderful — perhaps even preferable — everyday movement can take on beautiful qualities when performed in unison and with clarity and commitment. Examine the symmetries found in the music as well as using it to accompany movement.

7-5. Combining Symmetries in a Circle (10 minutes)

Have the students complete a similar chart showing the results of combining quarter turns. For example, the result of doing a 3/4 clockwise turn followed by another 3/4 clockwise turn is the same as a single 1/2 turn:

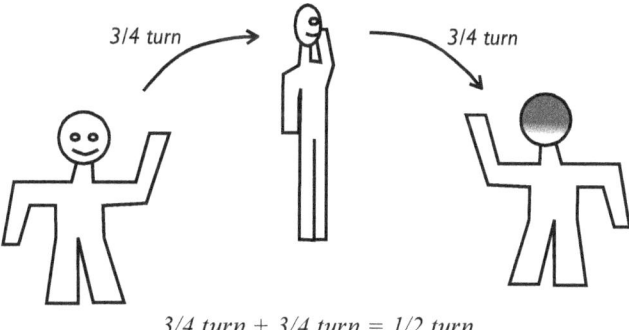

3/4 turn + 3/4 turn = 1/2 turn

Fill in the chart. Specify that all the turns are clockwise, and the numbers represent the number of quarter turns. Think of the 0 as representing either no turn or a full turn or 4 quarters (or any whole number of turns).

Quarter Turns		*Second turn*			
		0	1	2	3
First turn	0				
	1				
	2				
	3				2

The completed chart is:

Quarter Turns

	Second turn			
First turn	**0**	**1**	**2**	**3**
0	0	1	2	3
1	1	2	3	0
2	2	3	0	1
3	3	0	1	2

Patterns
- Again ask the class to make a list of patterns they see in this table.
- Which patterns are the same as those found in the line symmetry table? Which are different?
- Explain why the patterns are determined by the way the symmetries work.
- Ask the class to make a list of notions of quarter turns or quarter amounts with which they are familiar. For example, they may come up with quarter hours on the clock, 6 hour shifts during the day, 3 month seasons in the calendar, 4 quarts in a gallon, the four year election cycle or Olympics cycle, quarter dollars, and so on.

7-6. Reflection and Assessment

Assessing the dance
- Do the compositions created based on this material have clear beginnings, middles, and ends, or are they simply illustrations of the concepts? Encourage students to let their imaginations fly, even if that seems to lead them astray from the more technical ideas presented here.
- Do their movement phrases use symmetry and asymmetry in clear and interesting ways?
- Have they successfully explored symmetry and asymmetry?
- Can they see examples of symmetry in dances they watch and in other art forms?
- In chapter 6, Watch Your p's and q's, we described several other types of symmetries commonly used by choreographers: canon, opposition, reversal, retrograde, and inversion. What do the students think will happen when these are combined with each other?

Assessing the mathematics
- Do the students correctly distinguish the various types of symmetry?
- Can they correctly combine two kinds of symmetries and find the resulting symmetry?
- Can they find patterns in the tables and relate these to movement?
- Can they translate successfully from movement to notation and back?
- What are their reactions to their discoveries of patterns they see in this work?

Questions for discussion
- Investigate the different words used for turning and symmetry. For example, engineers might use the words pitch, roll, and yaw where we used cartwheel, somersault, and spin. Which corresponds to which? Are there other systems of words like this in common use?
- Think of real-life situations that involve combinations of two or more symmetries. Discuss how we can solve problems in these situations. Example: which way should we put a decal on the back window of a car so it looks correct when seen in the rear view mirror? Answering this question requires that we think about two reversals: the mirror, and looking through the window from either side. Another example: deciding which way to put an envelope in a printer so it prints address labels correctly.

7-7. Further Activities

Exploring other dance symmetries. In Chapter 6, *Watch Your p's and q's*, we described several symmetries in time that are commonly used in the dance world.
- **Canon.** Translation in time, in which a dancer does the same movements but later than another dancer.
- **Inversion.** Reversing the order of the movements, but not reversing the movements themselves.
- **Retrograde.** The movements are performed as if time were reversed.

We also detailed two spatial symmetries:
- **Opposition.** Usually refers to the arms having opposite orientation to the legs.
- **Reversal.** Movements to the front of the body done to the back, and vice versa.

We might add another symmetry in time:
- **Backward.** A sequence of movements are done in the same order, except that each individual movement is performed retrograde, reversed in time.

Investigate how these additional symmetries combine.
- How do the four symmetries in time — normal, inversion, retrograde and backward — combine? For example, if dancer B does the inversion of a sequence of movements by A, and dancer C does the retrograde of B's sequence, what will the relationship of C's sequence be to A's?
- Build a table that shows how these symmetries combine.
- Explore these symmetries in the same way as we investigated the others: have students work in groups and take turns "being the leader." In this case, since the symmetries are in time, one dancer will perform a phrase, and another will do the same phrase, or the inversion, retrograde, or backward of that phrase, a little later.
- Create a sequence of movements in groups of three or more dancers that further explore these symmetries in time.
- Explore opposition and reversal utilizing a similar sequence of activities.
- Explore ways to combine all the symmetries we have discussed. Create phrases that utilize a variety of symmetries, and show them to the class.
- The class should discuss the phrases both in terms of mathematical ideas as well as choreographic content.

Looking for symmetry in dance. Go to a library or dance teacher and check out or borrow a few dance videos. Watch the video(s) as a group and look for the uses of symmetry. There may be symmetries you not only recognize but can name. There also may be relationships between groups of dancers that feel as though they are symmetric, yet do not fit into the categories we have introduced in this book. As a class, try to define some of these new symmetries. When looking at these possible symmetries, ask yourselves: "What is the same? What is different?" Videos of folk and ethnic dances, movie musicals, or the works of choreographers like Alvin Ailey, George Ballanchine, Martha Graham, and Mark Morris are all fair game.

Moving through all the symmetries. In 6-7 Switching Symmetries we showed how pairs of dancers can switch smoothly between mirror and rotational symmetry, and between translation and glide symmetry. In this exercise we go a step further.

Divide the class into pairs. Challenge pairs of students to start in mirror symmetry and move through the other three symmetries (rotation and glide and translation) while always moving symmetrically. This is quite tricky. Hint: try turning 90° to the left or right, and explore what happens when the body takes a bilaterally symmetrical position. Bilateral symmetry occurs when the two halves of the body are mirror images of each other:

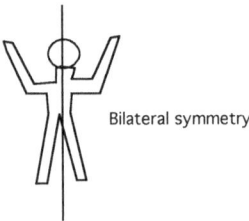

Bilateral symmetry

The partners may discover that it is possible to move from mirror symmetry, through bilateral symmetry, to either translation or rotation, but not to glide. The switch from mirror to translation is accomplished by moving to a position exhibiting bilateral symmetry, with both dancers facing one quarter turn to the side. Then the leader announces the switch and moves back to facing the front, away from the follower. The switch from mirror to rotation also involves first moving to a position of bilateral symmetry, but the students may remain facing each other the entire time. The switches involving glide are similar. This chart shows the possibilities:

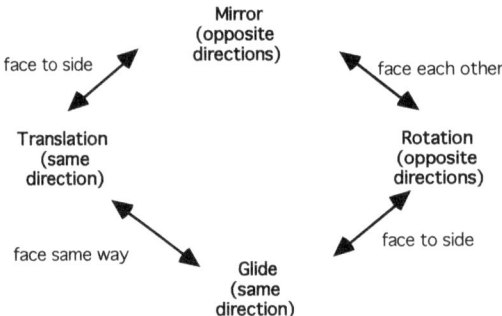

Aesthetics of symmetry. Architects have long used symmetry to convey a sense of order and ceremony. Facades of important government buildings are almost always symmetrical.
- In art and dance many people feel that precisely symmetrical compositions are dull and lifeless. What do students in the class think?
- Look at videotapes of dances. Find places where the dancers switched from one symmetry to another. How did they accomplish this?
- Read Doris Humphrey's chapter on symmetry and asymmetry in her book *The Art of Making Dances*, in which she criticizes the use of symmetry. Do students agree or disagree?
- Find a videotape of a dance by Doris Humphrey (one of the pioneers of American modern dance), and list the kinds of symmetries she used, and the transitions from one to another.

Modular and symmetry group arithmetic. The table for the sums of quarter turns is also known as the addition table, modulo 4. Sometimes this kind of arithmetic is known as clock arithmetic, because it is how we add hours on the face of a clock. Investigate these ideas using the resources given at the end of the chapter. The tables are themselves examples of symmetry group tables.
- Modular arithmetic and the operations of symmetry groups can get complex quickly. For example, ask students to try the activity with the doll using quarter turns instead of half turns.
- First students will have to decide whether to do the quarter turns using the original axis, or the new axis of the doll. Is a spin always a spin of a vertical axis of the body or of a vertical axis independent of the body?
- In the case of quarter turns, does the order of the turns matter?
- Try the turning exercise using one-third turns instead of quarter turns, and build a corresponding table.

Patterns in the symmetry charts. Students often ask why we put the four symmetries in the particular order translation, glide, reflection, and then rotation in the chart. What would happen if the order were switched? This is worth trying. (The patterns remain the same!) They might also try to invent "moving explanations" for the patterns they found in the chart that involve walking and moving through the symmetries, while talking about what is happening. Students might like to know that many of the patterns they find in the chart might be called "theorems" in a standard math book.

Complex Numbers. Another fascinating application of the quarter turns chart, for older students who have studied some algebra, involves complex numbers. This number system extends the real number system of positives and negatives, rational numbers and irrationals, to include square roots of negative numbers, which are called imaginary numbers. The number i is defined to be one of the square roots of negative one, and it has the property that i times i equals -1.

Unfortunately, in the traditional math curriculum, imaginary numbers are treated as bizarre and unreal, with no occurrence in the world. Ask students to fill in the chart at right, which is a multiplication table of the successive powers of i $1=i^0$, $i=i^1$, $-1=i^2$, and $-i=i^3$. Students will notice that the patterns are exactly those of the quarter turn chart. In other words, these "imaginary" numbers, and their products are actually a way of symbolizing what happens when we do quarter turns!

	Multiplying Complex Numbers		*Second number*			
			1	i	-1	$-i$
First number		1				
		i				
		-1				
		$-i$				

7-8. Resources

Holt, Michael, and Zoltan Dienes. *Let's Play Math.* New York: Walker and Company, 1973. A variety of movement games, some involving combining symmetry operations. See also other works by Zoltan Dienes.

Humphrey, Doris, edited by Barbara Pollack. *The Art of Making Dances.* New York: Grove Press, Inc., 1959. The classic work on how to choreograph dance, by one of the early pioneers of American modern dance. She had very strong opinions about the use of symmetry and asymmetry in dance.

Kinsey, L. Christine, and Teresa E. Moore. *Symmetry, Shape, and Space: An Introduction to Mathematics Through Geometry.* Emeryville, CA: Key College Publishing: 2002. A liberal arts math text based on symmetry, with lots of fascinating side-trips and connections to the arts.

Martin, George E. *Transformation Geometry, An Introduction to Symmetry.* New York: Springer-Verlag, 1982. An excellent mathematical reference.

Rosen, Joe. *Symmetry Discovered: Concepts and Applications in Nature and Science.* Dover Press, 1975. An accessible introduction to the ideas of symmetry.

Schattschneider, Doris. *Visions of Symmetry: Notebooks, Periodic Drawings, and Related Work by M. C. Escher.* W. H. Freeman & Co., 1992. The best reference for Escher's symmetry drawings, many of which appear for the first time in print. Meticulous mathematical analysis written by a mathematician with an eye for art.

Walser, Hans. *Symmetry.* Washington, DC: Mathematical Association of America: 2000. A free-ranging exploration of symmetry in nature and science.

7-9. Black-line Master — Twisted Addition

Combining Symmetries

	Second symmetry: B to C			
First symmetry: A to B	**T**	**G**	**M**	**R**
T				
G				
M				
R				

T = translation (p→p)   G = glide (p→b)   M = mirror (p→q)   R = rotation (p→d)

Quarter Turns

	Second turn			
First turn	**0**	**1**	**2**	**3**
0				
1				
2				
3				

0 = no turn (p→p)   1 = quarter turn (p→ᴅ)   2 = half turn (p→d)   3 = three quarters turn (p→ᴅ)

Math Dance with Dr. Schaffer and Mr. Stern • © 2001 Schaffer, Stern, Kim • www.mathdance.org

Chapter 8

Hand Figures
Making shapes with your hands, arms and body

Grades:	K–12
Time:	15–60 minutes
Concepts:	Math: Geometry, polygons, polyhedra, spatial visualization
	Dance: Dance with hands, ensemble, shape, transitions
Group size:	1–4
Space:	Requires clear floor
Materials:	Pencil and paper
Related activities:	Chapter 9 *String Figures*, chapter 10 *Stick Figures* (similar issues, different materials)
	Chapter 1 *How Many Ways to Shake Hands?* and Chapter 2 *Clap Your Name* (also uses hands)

This chapter and much of the chapter that follows (*String Figures*) focus on the hands and arms. Other than the face, the hands are the most articulate and expressive part of the human body. Polynesian dances, Native American dances, Spanish Flamenco, Cambodian classical court dances, and classical dance forms from India such as Bharatya Natyam are examples of dance forms from around the world that use elaborate hand movements and gestures. In many of these forms, hand movements represent specific ideas or things, such as water, happiness, or bull horns; sometimes, however, the gestures are purely abstract.

Though most exercises in this book are for the whole body, in this chapter students explore the surprising variety of geometric figures they can make with just their hands. They also handle imaginary shapes in space, and choreograph their hands as if the hands are dancers. These exercises help students develop their spatial visualization abilities and get a tactile sense for how different shapes are related. Students can work seated in chairs or sitting on the floor.

We have choreographed a number of dances for hands. Most recently the three authors choreographed and performed *Faux Paws*, a dance for eight hands performing on a video screen. In this video dance for eight hands, the appendages explore symmetries, curious shapes, sequences in canon, and movements that resemble aquatic animals.

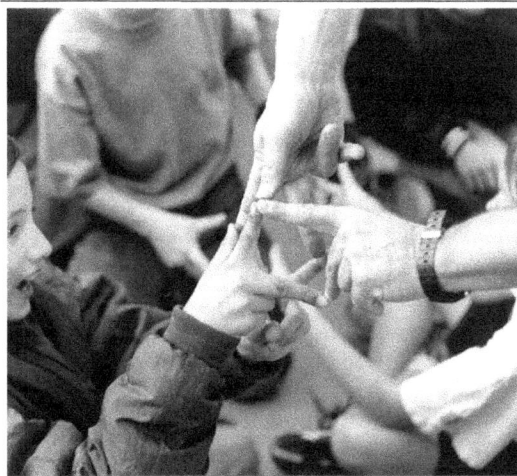

8–1. Hand Exercises (3-5 minutes)

When we first taught these exercises, we were reminded that the strength and flexibility of the hands takes time to develop. Here are some exercises to get hands warmed up. Make certain that students do not try to force their hands into the positions: the hands can be injured.
- Have students move their left hands in as many different ways as possible. Ask them, "Can you move one finger at a time? Two fingers? Notice how the fingers naturally move in sequence (for example, fanning the fingers). Now try with the right hand. Then with both hands." Words that might encourage contrasting motions include "smooth," "fan-like," "disjointed," and "sudden."
- Have students improvise shapes using both hands. Again they should work individually.
- Have students move their two hands so one hand is moving in a way that is opposite how the other hand is moving. Some pairs of opposite movement qualities include fast/slow, large/small, sudden/smooth, and straight/curved. Then ask them to switch which hand is doing which motion.
- Say, "Imagine your hands can talk to one another using movement. Have a conversation with your hands." Students may at first make a "mouth" with their hands, and use it to talk; this is a natural place to start. Encourage them to explore the movement more fully.

8–2. Shape Pass (3–5 minutes)

This improvisatory group exercise sensitizes students to making imaginary shapes with their hands.
- Ask students to get into groups of four. Number off in a circle, 1, 2, 3, 4.
- Student 1 pretends to hold a simple shape in the hands. Without speaking, handle the shape so everyone in the group can see exactly what the shape is. Show how big it is, where the corners are, how heavy it is, and so on. Carefully give the shape to student 2.
- Student 2 takes the shape from student 1, making sure to keep it the exactly same size and shape. Then change it into a new shape, say what it is, and hand it to student 3.
- The groups continue handing the shapes around. Keep finding new shapes and new ways to make the shapes. Feel free to use the arms, head or legs.

8–3. Hand Shape Shifting (5–10 minutes)

In this exercise students explore shapes they can make with their hands in small groups.
- Work in groups of four. Stand or sit in a circle.
- One student reaches into the center and makes a shape with her hands. The shape can be flat or dimensional, with fingers together or apart. Once the student has made a hand shape, she holds her hands still.
- A second student reaches into the center and adds onto the shape with his hands. Hands do not have to touch. Again, once the student has made a hand shape, he holds his hands still.
- Successive students keep adding to the hand shape until everyone in the group is participating. Then the first person removes her hands from the shape and places them in a new position. The second person removes his hands from the shape and places them in a new position. And so on.
- Notice the interesting variety of shapes that can be made with hands. Students may choose to continue patterns establish by previous students, or go strike off in new directions.

8–4. Hand Polyhedra (1–4 people)

These activities describe specific ways to make tetrahedra and cubes with fingers and arms, working in groups of 1 to 4 people. Each activity includes both specific directions and open-ended questions. Some of the shapes may be hard to perceive, since fingers are not precise building materials. We recommend you make straw models of the tetrahedron and cube, so students can see what they are trying to make. Having students make their own models is even better. See page 84 for instructions.

Two-person finger tetrahedron. Demonstrate this shape with a partner for the whole class before letting them try it.
- Students work in pairs. "Turn to face your partner. Put your thumbs together to make a straight line. Point your second and third fingers away from you and open them wide like two pairs of scissors. Notice that the four fingertips of your first and second fingers touch the four corners of a rectangle."
- "Turn to face your partner. One of you, not both, turn your hands sideways so your thumbs are pointing up and down.
- "Join the tips of your four fingers to the tips of your partner's fingers and see what shape you get. You may have to straighten out your fingers a bit to make the edges straight. See if you can find four triangles. This shape is a tetrahedron."
- "Now try separating all four hands a little so the hands (the corners of the tetrahedron) move apart. Bring your hands back together to make the tetrahedron. Keep moving your hands apart and together to make the tetrahedron breathe. Also allow all twelve fingers to collapse slowly in to the center and blossom out. How far you can separate your hands and still bring them back?"
- Further question: "Your fingertips join at six points. Visualize where those points are in space. If you joined these six points together, what shape would they make? Can you draw it?" Answer: octahedron.

Two-person cube. This cube is closely related to the two-person finger tetrahedron. Demonstrate this shape with a partner for the whole class before letting them try it.
- "Point your second and third fingers at your partner and open up the fingers wide like two pairs of scissors. Touch your fingertips to your partner's fingertips to make two diamonds."
- "Point your left and right thumbs at each other but don't let them touch. Raise your right elbow and lower your left elbow and let your hands turn with them."
- "Bring your hands together to touch your thumb tips to finger tips, completing the cube."
- "Now try separating all four hands a few inches, then bring them back together, to make the shape get bigger and smaller. Let the fingers collapse into the center and blossom out. See how far you can separate your hands and still get them back together."
- Further questions: "How could you make a tetrahedron or cube with four people? With six people? With more than six people? What other shapes can you make with your fingers? Can you draw pictures that help you remember the shapes you made and how you made them?"

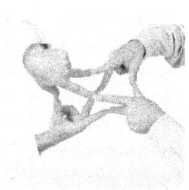

Two-person finger tetrahedron to cube. Once you have mastered the 2-person tetrahedron and the 2-person cube, you are ready for a dramatic transformation. You can present the transformation as a challenge for students to solve, or direct them step-by-step through the transformation.
- Challenge: "Can you figure out how to transform the tetrahedron smoothly into a cube and back?"
- Step-by-step: "Make the tetrahedron. Separate all four hands slightly so your thumbs no longer touch."
- "Pretend your two hands are grasping two shower knobs. Rotate both hands as if you were turning both knobs to the right, then to the left. One thumb

will move up while the other moves down."

- "Turn both hands clockwise to the right until your left index finger touches your right thumb tip, and your left thumb touches your right middle finger, forming a square. Your other first and second fingers point at your partner, not at each other! This is the same position your hands were in when you made a 2-person finger cube."
- "Join your hands to make a cube. Practice moving smoothly between the tetrahedron and cube."
- Further question: "Notice that in the tetrahedron each edge is made of two fingers, while in the cube each edge is made of just one finger. Can you guess what this means about the number of edges in the tetrahedron compared to the number of edges in the cube? Count the edges in the tetrahedron and the cube to check your guess." Answer: the cube has twice as many edges (12) as the tetrahedron (6).

One-person finger tetrahedron. This is an advanced way to make the tetrahedron. Some people lack the finger dexterity to do it well, so tell students that if they have trouble making this shape, they can watch someone else making it.

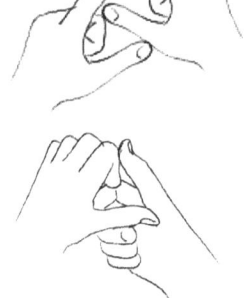

- Face away from the class and hold your hands over your head, so students see your hands from the same point of view they see their own hands.
- Make your hands into fists with palms pointing away from the class. Stick out your thumbs and forefingers. "Touch the tip of your left thumb to the base of your right thumb".
- Continue touching fingers. "Touch the tip of your right thumb to the second knuckle of your left index finger. Touch the tip of your left index finger to the second knuckle of your right index finger. Finally, curl your right index finger down to join the base of your left thumb."
- "Straighten your fingers and see if you can see all four triangles that make up the tetrahedron." You'll have to straighten out your fingers a bit, especially the knuckle of your index finger on both hands."
- "Now, keeping your fingers rigid, try moving your two hands away from each other, and turn your right hand so you are looking at the back of both hands. Notice that your hands make shapes that are mirror images of each other. Each hand makes three edges of the tetrahedron."
- "Can you reassemble your hands to make a tetrahedron?" This is an assembly puzzle using your own hands. Some people find this quite difficult and unfamiliar, because no fingertip touches any other fingertip in the final shape.
- Further question. "Because your two hands are mirror images of each other, you can pull your hands apart and twist your hands another way to make the tetrahedron another way. Can you figure out how?" Answer: move your hands apart, rotate your right hand so you are looking at the back of the hand, then rotate your left hand the same way your right hand was rotated, and move the hands back together. Start by touching the right thumb to the base of the left thumb.

8–5. Cubes in Space

Improvisation leads to dance sequences in this challenging exercise in spatial visualization.
- Have students work in groups of 3 or more. Each group pretends to hold a large cube a foot or two off the ground. "Move your hands to touch all the corners of the cube until you all agree on exactly how big the cube is and where it is in space. Be sure the cube is small enough that you can reach every point on its surface."
- "Move your hands slowly along the edges of the cube. Keep the cube still. Explore all the edges."

- "Move your hands along the faces of the cube. Be sure to keep your body outside the cube. Explore all the faces, letting your hands bend around the edges as they move from face to face. Try to make the cube as vivid as possible in your mind."
- "Explore other ways to move around the cube, while keeping some part of your body in contact with the surface of the cube at all times."
- "As a group, try transforming the cube in different ways, such as turning it, shrinking it, throwing it or crumpling it."
- "Based on your explorations, create a series of movements that starts with no one touching the cube, reaches a point where everyone is touching the cube, and ends with everyone transforming the cube in some way. Rehearse your sequence until you can do it without hesitation, then perform it for the rest of the class."

8–6. Dances with Hands

In this composition exercise, students invent dance sequences with the hands, and perform them for each other. Divide the class into groups of four, if they are not already in such groups. (If necessary, groups of three or five will work well too.) The students may be seated in a circle on the floor.

- Ask each group to make a sequence of at least three shapes with the hands. They may use polyhedral shapes from previous exercises, or create new ones.

- Have students figure out a way to move through the sequence of these shapes, taking care to find interesting transitions between them. Have students rehearse the shapes so the sequence can be performed confidently and without the need for verbal cues.
- Students may want to add verbal sound effects once they have settled on a sequence and rehearsed it. Or they may want to wait until the sequence is choreographed and try adding recorded music to it.
- Remind students to find a clear beginning and ending for their hand shape study. Investigate and play with altering the movement qualities of the hands as they create the group's shapes. The hands may interlock, or remain apart. Hands may join together all at once or move into and out of the center one at a time. Play with the order in which hands enter or leave the shapes, and the qualities of motion the hands exhibit. The main thing to look for is movement that keeps the viewers' focus on the hands.
- Once the hand dances are rehearsed, make a performance order. The dances are best viewed by having the audience gather around the circle of seated performers and watch from above.

8–7. Reflections and Assessment

Dance
Encourage the students to make movement that keeps the viewers focus on shape. Ask the observers to comment on the following criteria.
- **Clarity.** Do dancers move with clarity and commitment, or are they tentative and unclear?
- **Movement quality.** Do the dancers use an appropriate range of movement qualities (slow/fast, tense/relaxed, big/small, linear/circular) that enhances the clarity of the shapes, or are movements inappropriate and distracting?
- **Composition.** Does the performance have a clear beginning and end, and sense of thematic unity and development?
- **Focus on shapes.** Is the viewer's attention clearly drawn to the hands (or whatever part of the body is relevant to making shapes), or is the focus unclear?
- **Invention.** Does the hand dance exhibit creativity? Is it humorous? Does it tell a story? Are the sound effects supportive of the idea of the piece and the movement of the hands?

Mathematics
- **Polyhedra**. Are the students able to name the polyhedra studied in this chapter: cube and tetrahedron. Do they know, or can they visualize, how many edges, vertices, and triangles or squares each has?
- **Visualization**. Have their three-dimensional visualization skills increased as a result of this work? Can they visualize a three-dimensional shape and draw it in the air, or rotate it in their minds?
- **Recording**. Have the students attempt to create a record in words and pictures of their hand dances. Are the records detailed enough that they can use them to help remember the dances a day or a week later? Are they clear enough that another group can use the record to recreate the dance?
- **Variation**. Vary the constructions slightly: ask the groups to make a four-person cube; two interlocking tetrahedra; an octahedron. It may be useful to have straw and paper-clip models available for the students to look at as they do this work.

Discussion
- The brain uses a large portion of its neurons for motor skills, and a large portion of that is used for the hands. Why?
- Ask the class to make a list of what the hands can do that the feet cannot. For instance, hands have opposable thumbs, each digit may be used independently (try typing a message with the toes!), they have sensory capabilities, and they have the ability to remember and recreate enormously complex muscle patterns (a violin sonata, heart surgery, knitting a sweater). The sensory and controlling mechanisms require oodles of neurons dedicated to these tasks.
- Everyone knows how to count to 10 on their fingers. How could we count from 1 to 100 on our two hands? What other mathematics can we do on our hands?

8–8. Further Activities

Hands as expression. At the beginning of this chapter, we mention dance forms that use the hands as an area of primary focus. Choose one of these dance forms and research what some of the hand positions or movements mean. Compare these dance gestures to gestures we have in our culture. Are there any similarities? Differences? Make a list of gestures that have meaning in our culture. If you can, compare them to non-dance gestures of another culture. Again, look for differences and similarities. Watch someone talking and look for hand gestures. Why do most people accompany verbal statements with hand, face and body gestures? What does that say about human communication? Why are the hands so important in communication?

Here are several ways students can create dances using just hands. The authors have choreographed dances for our stage performances using all of these methods.

In a box. Use a cardboard box that is about two feet wide in all directions. Place the box on a chair and turn it so the opening faces the audience. Cut several holes around the sides and top that let performers insert their arms up to their elbows. See what shapes they can make inside the box. Find interesting ways to add and take away hands from the shapes. The box acts like a miniature stage that showcases the hands. They can make the effect even stronger by lighting the inside of the box and hiding the bodies of the performers behind a curtain or wall, and wearing white gloves.

For a video camera. Point a video camera straight down at a black tabletop, and have people move their hands just above the table. Try making shapes with two or more hands. Play with the way hands enter and leave the frame. Experiment with different types of motion, both slow and fast. If performers want to use their entire bodies to make shapes, not just the hands, try suspending a video camera from the ceiling and have them lie on the floor. Try arranging several dancers in a circle with heads toward the center, and have them wave their arms and legs. This creates a kaleidoscopic pattern similar to those in old Busby Berkeley movie musicals. They should practice until they can synchronize their movements.

From behind a curtain. Cut a pattern of vertical slits in an old sheet. Hang the sheet from the ceiling or a door frame. Dancers stand behind the sheet and push their arms through the sheet up to the elbows. They can try making shapes with their forearms. Experiment with different ways to move the fingers, hands and arms. Play with the way arms enter and exit through the holes. It's hard for performers to see what they are doing, so have someone watch the movements and give feedback, or practice in front of a mirror and peek through holes in the sheet.

Beyond hands. People's hands vary in length, strength and flexibility. Some students may not be able to use their hands, but can still use other parts of their body. We once choreographed a piece for four performers using only our faces, and filmed it. Instead of moving our arms and legs, we moved our eyes and mouths. It was one of the most challenging pieces we have ever performed!

Here are other mathematical topics the class can explore using their hands.

Mathematical hand signs. Invent hand signs for mathematical concepts you are learning in class, such as positive and negative, or triangle and square. Inventing a mathematical hand sign is an interesting exercise in understanding the essence of an idea. Using the signs in class makes the concepts more memorable, and allows the teacher to poll the entire class at once and be able to see what each student is answering.

Chisenbop (chee-zen-bop). This is a Korean method of doing arithmetic on the fingers. The left hand represents the tens place, and the right hand represents the ones place. On each hand raise from zero to four fingers for the numbers 0 to 4, and also raise or lower the thumb for the number 5. For instance, to represent the number 73, raise two fingers and a thumb on the left hand, and three fingers but not the thumb on the right hand. Doing calculations in Chisenbop is similar to using an abacus, with fingers in place of beads. How can addition and subtraction be done in Chisenbop? For more information, see Chisenbop resources at the end of this chapter.

Knots. The branch of mathematics that studies knots is called topology. Topology is like geometry, except shapes are allowed to be bent and stretched, as long as they don't break. For instance, a basic theorem of topology is that a knotted loop cannot be transformed into an unknotted loop without breaking the loop.
- "Join hands with two other people to make a circle. Can you join hands to make a knotted loop?"
- "Can you change the knotted loop into an unknotted loop? You can't do this without letting go of your hands, but it is fun to try."
- "Can you make other sorts of knots with your hands and fingers?"
- "What knots can you make with two people? One person? Four or more people?"

8–9. Resources

Chisenbop. Korean system for doing arithmetic on your fingers, closely related to the abacus. Books on Chisenbop all seem to be currently out of print. There is a good tutorial on the web at: http://klingon.cs.iupui.edu/~aharris/chis/chis.html

Cromwell, Peter R. *Polyhedra*. Cambridge, England: Cambridge Univ. Press, 1997. A comprehensive look at the history and theory of polyhedra.

George Hart's Pavilion of Polyhedreality. An elaborate online art gallery of polyhedron models, with references to books and other web sites.
http://euch3i.chem.emory.edu/proposal/www.li.net/~george/pavilion.html. Also see Vladimir Bulatov's polyhedron gallery at http://www.physics.orst.edu/~bulatov/polyhedra/.

Michael Moschen approaches juggling with the eye of a sculptor and the compositional sense of a choreographer to create intricate solo performances that are both imaginative and bewildering His work is full of mathematical patterns and inventive use of props. See his web site http://www.michaelmoschen.com, as well as "Michael Moschen: In Motion", a one hour videotape from the PBS Dance in Amerca series, 1991, available through Amazon.com. The video includes both performances and a look at his creative process.

Labyrinth (1986). This visually imaginative feature-length movie includes a sequence where several pairs of hands against a black background come together to make a talking face.
Straw Polyhedra. Good lesson plan on the web at:
http://www.math.nmsu.edu/breakingaway/Lessons/straw/straw.html. Also see Soda Straw Tensegrity Structures at: http://euch3i.chem.emory.edu/proposal/www.li.net/~george/virtual-polyhedra/straw-tensegrity.html.

Pilobolus is an American modern dance company that makes astonishing shapes out of human bodies. Their web site http://www.pilobolus.com includes many images from their performances. Also see "Pilobolus — Monkshood's Farewell", a one hour videotape from the PBS Dance in America series, 1977, available from Music Video Distributors or Amazon.com. Includes four pieces, and is appropriate for classrooms.

Polydron. Polyhedral building kit that uses plastic panels in the shapes of triangles, squares, pentagons, etc. Particularly durable and suitable for younger hands. Now includes spherical and open-frame pieces. The full product line is available through www.polydron.com.

Zome System, by Zometool, Inc. An excellent though expensive construction set for making stick figure polyhedra, including cubes and tetrahedra as well as icosahedra and dodecahedra. Comes with durable colorful plastic sticks and connectors. Available through Amazon.com. See http://www.zometool.com for the complete story, including lesson plans, and the Zome Geometry Book.

8–10. How to Make a Soda Straw Tetrahedron

Materials:
6 plastic drinking straws
12 paper clips. The clips should be the right size to squeeze snugly into an end of the straw.

Directions:
- Bend each paper clip open into an S shape that lies flat on a table.
- Insert a paper clip, big end first, into each end of each straw, leaving only a small loop protruding.
- Join pairs of straws by pulling a clip out halfway out of one straw, hooking it to the clip at the end of the other straw, then pushing the clip back in.
- To make a tetrahedron, first make a triangle, join an extra straw to each corner of the triangle, then gather the three open ends at the top and join them.
- Of course cubes, octahedra, and other polyhedra can also be made out of straws and paper clips. Remember, two clips are needed for each straw. The cube model will tend to bend and fall over (and can be flexed into interesting shapes), but models that are all triangles will hold themselves rigid.
- It's easy to take these models apart and pack them flat, which is good for storage and travel. To make more permanent models, try threading string through the straws. The models are light enough to hang from the ceiling by a single thread.

CHAPTER 9
Figures in String
Exploring geometry with loops of string

Grades:	2-12
Time:	40-60 minutes
Groups:	2, 3, and 4
Materials:	Handout (page 95) for each student, loop of string for each group
Space:	Relatively clear space — some activities may be done in chairs; tables or desks may hinder.
Concepts:	Math: Symmetry, visual thinking, Dance: dance with props
Prerequisites:	None
Related Activities:	Chapter 8 *Hand Figures*, chapter 10 *Stick Figures* (similar issues, different materials)

String figures, the imaginative designs created with simple loops of string, are found among the world's most ancient cultures. A few — Jacob's Ladder, Cat's Cradle, or Witch's Broom, for example — will be familiar to many, but the world's lore contains thousands of other beautiful and complex designs. In Western culture these figures seem to be an art form practiced primarily by children. The combination of manual dexterity with the learning of complex pattern and sequencing seem to go "hand in hand" at that age. In many other cultures string play is a lifelong avocation and we believe it is an art form that should not be lost. Emphasizing its performance and geometric elements takes string figures naturally into the realms of dance and mathematics.

We began our interest in string figures when we heard that local Santa Cruz, California expert Greg Keith had been teaching dancers to perform them with giant loops of rope and we invited him to join us at a rehearsal. We progressed from his instruction to learning them from books, to inventing our own three-dimensional string polyhedra. One of our outreach performances for the schools now includes giant traditional string figures, string polyhedra, and playful dances with loops of thick rope.

String figures are a great example of an activity that children and adults can share. We have seen children as young as 6 years old learn string figures and teach them to their parents. We have had success working with the string activities in this book with second graders and with college students. For example, both second graders and adults found it challenging to discover how two people working together could make a string tetrahedron or a five-pointed star with a single loop of string. But the adults were able to make the abstract connections between the formation of the tetrahedron and what are called "Euler circuit problems" described below. We present here a variety of group activities for all ages exploring the playful possibilities in a loop of string.

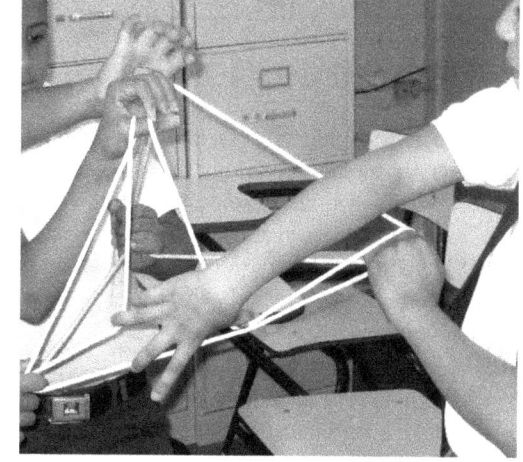

Our geometric string figures related to traditional string play, which often functions as expressive art form in the cultures in which they originate. An interesting analogy might be made with the Japanese art of paper folding, called "origami." Traditional origami is flat, involves shapes reminiscent of animals or people, and is made from a single sheet of paper. Traditional string figures also often have these characteristics. However contemporary origami includes many beautiful three-dimensional geometric constructions, often of polyhedra, and often involving numerous modules all of the same shape, analogous to the purely geometrical three-dimensional string figures in this chapter.

9-1. Making Loops (preparation)

Throughout these activities, students will use a loop of string that stretches the width of a typical student's "wingspan." Students work with the loops in groups of two or four, so they need only one string for every two or four students. If there is time we recommend making a loop for every student so students can explore making solo shapes as well; after doing these activities many students will want to take the loops home so they can show the shapes to friends and family. Wingspan is about the same as height, so double the average student's height to get the length of string needed for each loop. Younger students will need about 7 or 8 feet of string per loop, older students about 10 or 11 feet. Err on the side of making the loops a little too big.

We recommend 1/8 inch thick cotton or braided nylon string (the braiding makes it more flexible). This is about twice as thick as average household string, which breaks or unravels too easily. Avoid clothesline or other stiff string. Do not use twine, which tends to unravel and does not slide easily against itself.

To join the ends of nylon string, melt them in a candle flame, and then roll the melted ends together. Do this outdoors, as the fumes are not healthy to breathe, and wear thick gardening gloves while rolling the hot melted ends together so as not to burn the hands. The ends of cotton string may be joined with a short rectangle of duct tape. Roll the tape cylindrically around the joined ends. Regular transparent or masking tape is not strong enough. Duct tape, as well as different sorts of string are available in hardware stores.

Melt the ends of nylon rope together and wear gloves while rolling the melted ends together.

Or tape the ends of the rope together with duct tape.

Safety note: Some of the traditional figures involve wrapping the string around the neck; be wary of children doing this! Also ask them not to put their full weight on the string, or to tangle loops together. When students are done with the strings, ask them to "fold" them in half a couple times and tie a loose overhand knot in them; this prevents strings from getting tangled in storage.

9-2. Body Polygons (5-10 minutes)

In this activity students work individually to create geometric shapes with their arms and body. Make sure students are spread throughout the space and have room to move their arms freely. If working in a classroom, have students stand up and move chairs to the side of the room.
- Ask students to "make a circle with your arms."
- "Transform it into a triangle. Try making triangles with different parts of your body. Make the largest triangle possible. Make the smallest triangle possible. Try to make an isosceles triangle. Try to make an equilateral triangle."
- "Make a four-sided shape (a quadrilateral). Name the body parts used for the sides. Try to make a rectangle. Try to make a square."
- "Make a pentagon. Consider what parts of the body are the sides."
- "Go back to the circle. The circle can also be considered a polygon with straight sides, because the forearms and upper arms are more straight than curved. How many sides does the "circle" have?"

9-3. Create a Movement Sequence (5-10 minutes)

In this activity, students create sequences of shapes, explore transitions, and perform them. Have students work in pairs, which allows many more ways to make shapes.
- Have students find as many other ways to make a triangle or quadrilateral with the body as possible. Use the arms, legs, chest, feet, and hands.
- Ask students, "Can you make a shape that we haven't mentioned? It does not even have to be a shape that has a name!"
- "Try tipping the shapes into different planes." For example, if a student is making a triangle which is parallel to the floor, can it be tilted? Remember, there are a number of ways to tilt a object. For example, one's right arm moves down and the left moves up, or the hands move up and the chest moves down. How does changing the plane of the shapes affect the whole body?
- "Try making the shape turn or spin. Try stepping through the shape."
- "Make up a sequence of three shapes and move from one shape to the next in an interesting way." Any of the shapes made so far are fair game. The transition from one shape to the next can be done many ways. As a class discuss a few approaches. For example, arms, chest and torso may move together; or they may be moved separately. The transition may be tense or bound, with muscles taut, or it may be light and relaxed. After discussing approaches to transitions, encourage students to play with the options. It is perfectly fine if the geometric shapes are released during the transitions. Transitions may be needed for all types of movements and shapes.
- Demonstrate the sequences. Groups may perform individually, or if time is short or students are shy, three or four might perform their creations at once. As a class discuss what the movement sequences looked like. Which parts were most interesting, and why?

9-4. String Polygons (10-15 minutes)

In this exercise students begin to explore simple geometric ideas with loops of string. As some of the shapes require different levels, students may sit in chairs if necessary. Make sure desks are out of the way, so they do not impede movement.
- Divide students into groups of four. (Alternatively, many of the exercises in this chapter can be done by pairs of students sharing one loop.)
- Hand one loop to each group.
- When students receive their string loops some may immediately begin to demonstrate traditional string figures that they know, like Cat's Cradle, Jacob's Ladder, or Witch's Broom. As with any manipulative, this initial play can be helpful. If there is time, you might want to allow those who know figures to demonstrate one or two.

Now try making polygons.
- "Make a square with the loop, with each person holding a different corner."
- Demonstrate how to hold a corner of the string by making a loop with the thumb and forefinger. Holding the string this way allows the string to slide easily through the fingers. Caution students against grasping the string; allow it to sit in the loop of the fingers. This will allow smooth transitions between shapes.
- "Transform the square into a triangle." One person in each group may want to drop out and watch during the next few exercises. "Make an isosceles triangle. Change its shape but keep it isosceles. Make an equilateral triangle. How can you tell it is equilateral?" One answer: check pairs of edges to make sure they have equal length by pivoting them toward each other until they coincide.
- "Make a right triangle. Change its shape but keep it a right triangle. Transform the triangle into a rectangle. Can you change the dimensions of the rectangle while keeping it a rectangle?"

- "Make a parallelogram that is not a rectangle. Change its shape but keep it a parallelogram. Make a trapezoid that is not a parallelogram."
- "Transform your loop into a 4-sided figure that does not sit in the plane (note: some people insist this should not be called a quadrilateral.)"
- Ask students if they discovered what some of the tricks are for handling the string. For example, holding the string in a loop made with the thumb and index finger takes concentration. It is easy to forget to keep that pressure between the thumb and index finger, letting the string drop away. But at the same time, one must keep the arms and torso relaxed, or else it can become difficult to move. Discuss ways to practice the tricks and techniques of handling string.

9-5. Transformations with Polygons (10-20 minutes)

     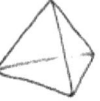

Making polygons. In this activity, students explore crossing parts of the strings and creating more complex shapes.
- Again, each group of four students works with one loop. Draw the shapes above, one at a time, on a chalkboard, or hand out the diagram. Challenge the groups to make the shapes with their loop of string.
- What other shapes can be made with one loop and four people?
- Which of the shapes can be made without any doubled strings? Answer: all but the last three. See the note on Euler circuits below.

Transforming polygons. Here are some challenges based on particular shapes.
- Have students make a pentagon. Then have them make a pentagram (five-pointed star). Challenge students to flex the pentagon so that it becomes a pentagram. This may be easier of you draw a picture on the board for everyone to see, or if you ask students to trace a five-pointed star in the air as if they were drawing it. Flexing the pentagon into a star often involves handing one's loop to a person on the other side of the group.
- Once the transformation from pentagon to five pointed star has been solved, have student find a way to change smoothly from the pentagon to the five-pointed star and back. Practice the transformation until it can be repeated reliably keeping the string taut at all times. Have groups perform their pentagram transformation for the rest of the class.
- Make a hexagon, then heptagon (seven sides), then octagon. Where do we often see octagons? (One answer: stop signs!) Find an interesting way to smoothly change a square into an octagon, back into a square, or a triangle into a hexagon, back into a triangle.
- Make a square with a cross in the middle of it: Is it possible to do this without any of the strings being doubled? (Answer: no — again see the math note below on Euler Circuits.)
- Lay the square-plus-cross flat in the horizontal plane, and pull one of the four outside up above the others. If this can be done without tangling the strings, the result should be a tetrahedron.
- Ask students if they discovered tricks and techniques for creating these shapes. For example, should one move quickly or slowly? Is it easier to keep the string away from the torso by extending the arms, or nearer the torso?

Dancing with polygons. If time allows, have students develop their string polygons into dances.
- Have each group make a sequence of three shapes using their loop of string. The shapes should be oriented vertically so they can be seen by an audience viewing the shapes from the side. One shape should involve all students in the group, the others can be made with fewer students, even just one.
- Create a way to move smoothly through all three shapes. Rehearse the sequence so it can be performed without hesitation.
- Here are some guidelines for creating dances. How does the sequence begin and end? How do body shapes complement the string shapes? What happens during the transition from one shape to the next? What do the students who are not involved in making a shape do? Return to the movement sequences in section 9-2 and have students incorporate some of the new shapes into their dances. Make up shapes that use the newly introduced examples of crossing strings, involve three dimensionality, or use the shapes exactly as presented above.
- View the dances and discuss.

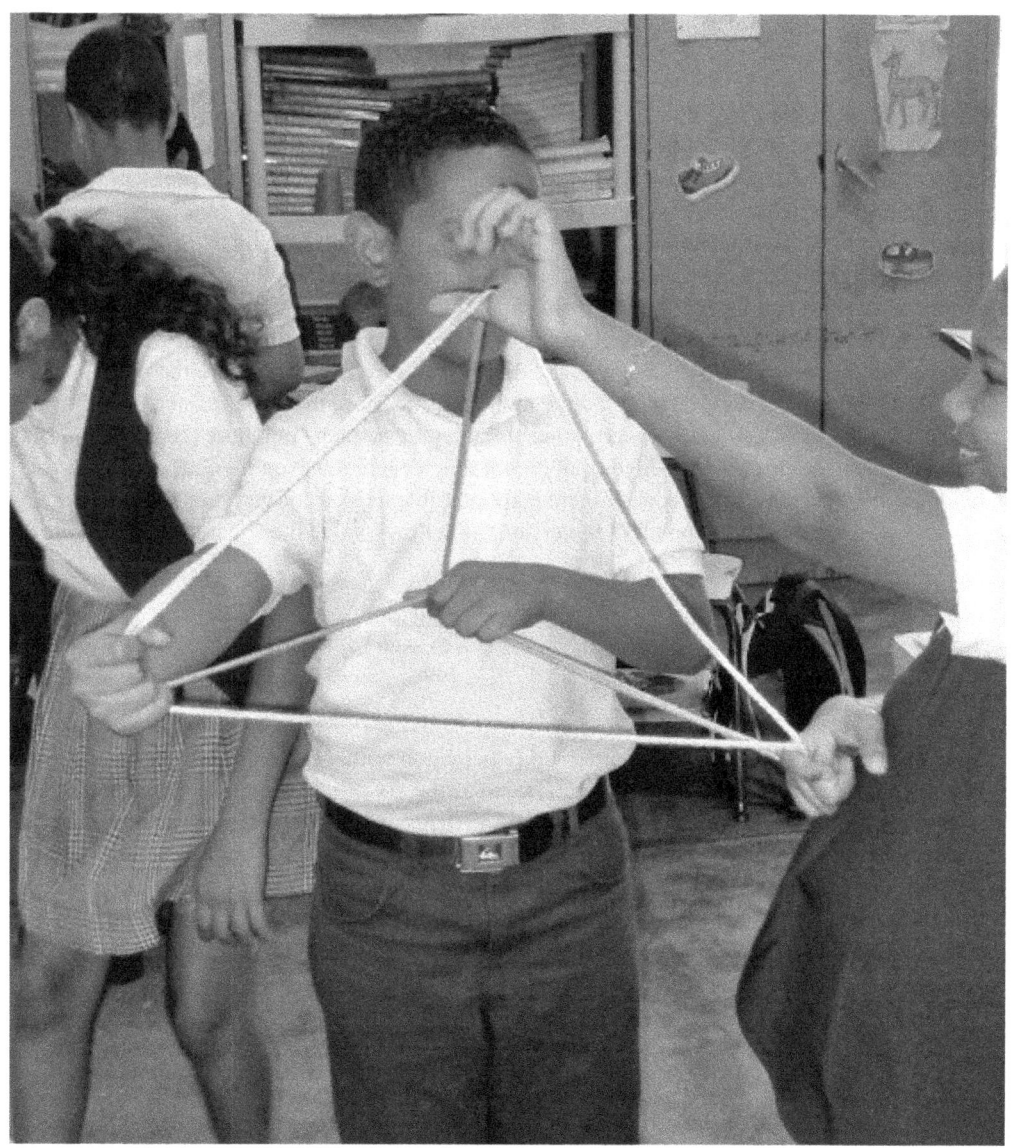

Math note: Euler circuits

Some of the questions we asked deal with whether the various polyhedra can be constructed without doubling the string along edges. This question is based on a classical mathematical problem first investigated by Swiss mathematician Leonhard Euler (1707-1783, pronounced "oiler") in the context of a "bridge-walking" question.

It seems the people of the town of Konigsberg (now Kalingrad) were puzzled as to whether they could traverse a series of bridges and islands and return to their starting point, having crossed each bridge exactly once. The diagram below shows a "Bridges of Tetrahedrasberg" problem similar to that confronting the people of Konigsberg (the actual puzzle differed only slightly):

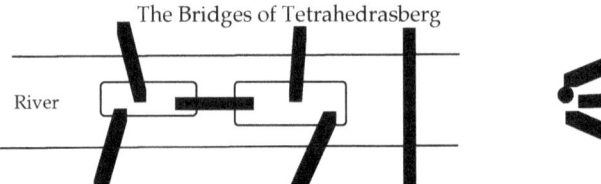
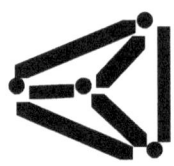

Euler noticed that in a problem like this the four land masses can be considered vertices, and the six bridges joining them, edges. The problem is now the same as that of trying to cover the tetrahedral map on the right with one loop of string, without doubling any edges. Yet another way of stating the problem is to ask whether you can draw the tetrahedral map in one continuous line without lifting your pencil or retracing any lines, and return to the starting point. Such paths are known as "Euler circuits." From this and similar problems were born the modern mathematical fields of graph theory and topology.

Euler noticed that if a continuous loop of string were to enter a vertex, it must also leave it, so that the total number of enterings and leavings at each vertex must be even. But in this map all vertices have an odd number of such "entrances and exits," known as the **degree** of the vertex. Therefore the problem cannot be solved unless some of the edges are covered by the loop of string more than once. Since each extra traversal of an edge affects 2 vertices by adding one extra degree at each, and there are a total of 4 vertices, the best we can do is to double 2 of the edges that do not touch each other (on the left, below). It can also be done by doubling 3 or more of the edges (4 and 6 are possible degrees of vertices, 1,3, and 5 are not...why?), and students may find one of these versions when they solve the square-plus-cross problem.

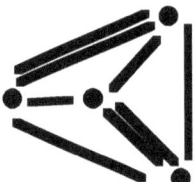
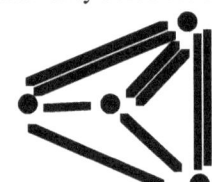

The same kind of analysis shows that the pentagram (a pentagon with a 5-pointed star inscribed) has 5 vertices that are all of even degree, the octahedron (same as the six-pointed star) has 6 that are all even, and the cube has 6 that are all odd. It turns out that when all vertices are even, the figure can always easily be covered with one loop with no doubling, and that explains why the pentagram and octahedron can be so constructed. In general a connected figure with n odd-degree vertices can be drawn in *n*/2 continuous paths without lifting the pencil off the paper inside a path, and without doubling any edges. Challenge for more advanced students: can they explain why *n* must always be an even number?

9-6. String Polyhedra (10-15 minutes)

   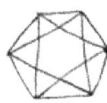 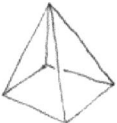  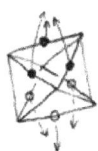 

Making polyhedra. The next few exercises are directed at constructing specific three-dimensional geometric shapes. If you prefer, you can draw the shapes or show models and challenge students to discover their own methods of making these shapes.
- Again, each group of four students works with one loop. Draw the pictures above on a chalkboard, one at a time, or hand out the diagram. Challenge the groups to make the shapes with their loops of string.
- What other three-dimensional forms can be made with one loop and four people?
- Which of the shapes can be made without any doubled strings? Answer: the "hypertetrahedron" (a tetrahedron with an additional point in the middle, also called the 5-simplex. It may be collapsed into the plane to form the pentagram.) and the octahedron. See math note above on Euler Circuits for details.

Transforming polyhedra. Here is one way to make all of the shapes in sequence. Have one group of four people sitting or standing in a circle demonstrate, then have others duplicate what they did:

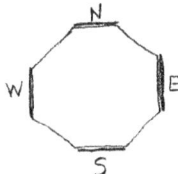 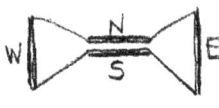 

1. Each of the four people, labeled N, E, S and W in this diagram, holds two adjacent vertices.

2. The north and south people bring their hands together at the top, and one person takes the strings from the other.

3. The east and west people do the same, bringing their hands together at the bottom, one person taking the strings from the other. Voila: **tetrahedron**!

 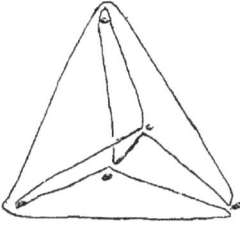 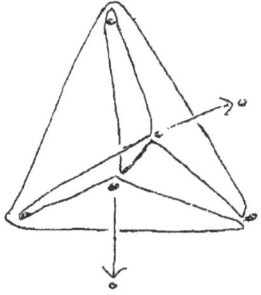

4. Notice which of the string edges of the tetrahedron are doubled. If a fifth hand pulls two of the doubled strings together into the middle of the tetrahedron (see diagram)...

5. ...a new polyhedron called the **hypertetrahedron** (or sometimes the 4-dimensional tetrahedron) results. Notice that each vertex has a string going to each of the other vertices.

6. If all vertices are now pulled to the "outside," and the figure is flattened into the plane, the result will be a...

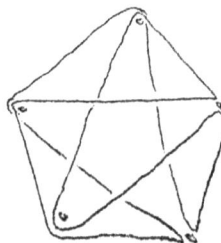 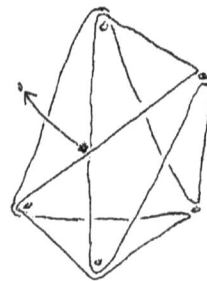 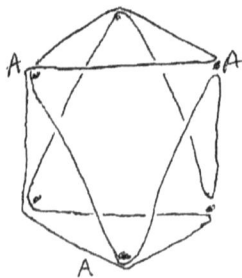

7. ...**pentagon with a five-pointed star** in the middle, known as the **pentagram**.

8. If someone grabs a pair of strings where they cross inside the pentagram and pulls it to the outside, the result should be a ...

9. ...**six-pointed star inside a hexagon**. In some cases three of the vertices will lie above the other three. If the three vertices labeled A in this diagram are raised upwards the result is an...

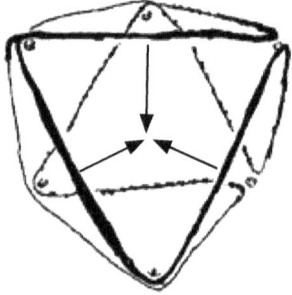 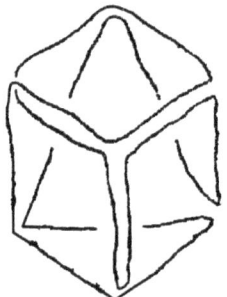 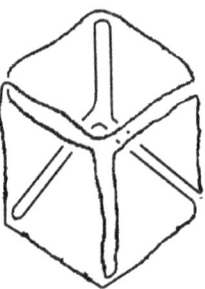

10. ...**octahedron**. Notice that this figure has no doubled strings. To transform an octahedron into a cube, a fourth person gathers the midpoints of the three sides of the top triangle with one hand...

11. ...into a point and pulls the point up. The other hard gathers the midpoints of the three sides of the bottom triangle into a point with the other hand...

12. ... and pulls down. Behold: **a cube** standing on one vertex!

Math and dance note: Polyhedra

Polyhedra are the building blocks of solid geometry, the same way triangles and quadrilaterals are the building blocks of planar geometry. Polyhedra are three-dimensional objects composed of polygons that enclose a single region of space. The edges of the polyhedron are formed where exactly two polygons share an edge, and the vertices are where three or more edges come together. Students can be asked to construct models of polyhedra out of straws and paper clips, as described in section 8-12, or even toothpicks stuck into gumdrops. They should look for everything that can be counted: numbers of faces, edges, vertices, edges per face, and edges per vertex, for example, and should learn to recognize the polyhedra.

Polyhedral symmetries and how they relate to human movement were studied by the movement analyst Rudolf Laban (1879-1958) and his followers. Laban developed the form of dance notation that is currently most popular, known as Labanotation. He was particularly fascinated by the icosahedron (made up of twenty triangles), and placed its twelve vertices around the body: two each above and below, two each in front and back, and two each to either side, as shown below. Note that six of the pairs of vertices and the corresponding six edges of the icosahedron lie in faces of a surrounding cube. He also imagined the dancer standing inside the octahedron so that its six vertices were in the centers of the square faces of the cube. (Note: in our drawing we have placed the icosahedron rotated 90° from the orientation in which Laban's followers usually draw it.)

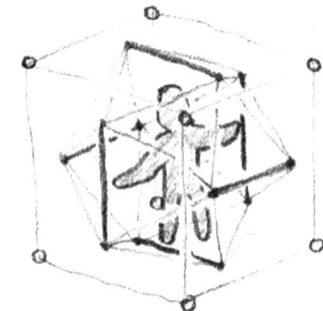

9-7. Dances with Polyhedra (10-15 minutes)

In this exercise students develop their string polyhedra into dances.
- Have each group choose a polyhedron from their explorations in 9-5. Find a way to make the shape so it can be seen by an audience viewing the shape from the side. (Note: if the string/rope polyhedra are rotated slightly the audience will be able to perceive its three-dimensional form more easily.)
- Experiment with different ways to smoothly form and unform the shape.
- Create a movement sequence that starts with one person holding the string, reaches a point where the whole group holds the string to make a polyhedron, and ends with one person again holding the string.
- Create a way to move smoothly through all three shapes. Rehearse the sequence so it can be performed without hesitation.
- Here are some guidelines for creating polyhedron dances. How does the sequence begin and end? How do body shapes complement the string shapes? Try to keep the audience's attention focused on the string and how the shapes change. Consider what the students who are not involved in making a shape do, such as: make similar shapes with their body, extend the shape, move around the shape, prepare to make the next shape, manipulate the shape.
- View the dances and discuss.
- A difficult but interesting variation is to perform the movement sequence without the string. This requires a great deal of concentration and the ability to accurately visualize shapes in space.

9-8. Assessment and Reflection

Assessing the dance
- Did dancers perform with energy and commit to their movements, without hesitation?
- Did groups perform with a coherent sense of ensemble?
- Were the shapes clear? Did the performers move in a way that kept the attention on the string shapes? Were the string shapes held taut when necessary?
- Were the transformations between shapes explored thoroughly and with imagination?

Refining the dance
Here are ways to push students to take their dances further.
- If a group solves one of the construction problems in a particularly clever, succinct or surprising way, have them rehearse it so that they can redo it quickly and efficiently.
- Ask students to use more of the body in the construction process: swing arms through large arcs, change levels, rotate themselves and the figure, carry the figure so that the entire class can see it.
- For performances for larger audience, ask students to rework their dances with thicker pieces of string or rope that are visible at a distance.
- Play music and see if they can carry out the construction in a way that is supported by the music. These are all movement performance problems even if the result does not at first look like a "dance."

Assessing the mathematics
Most of the activities in this chapter can be done by students from kindergarten to college.
- The warm-up and initial exercises are designed to review the definitions of simple geometric shapes, and to make distinctions between them. Can students identify and name the shapes they make?
- Can students distinguish and make the requested shapes, e.g. right versus isosceles triangle?
- Can students identify and count the vertices, edges and faces of polyhedra?
- Have students draw the shapes they invent, especially in order to record dances they create. Include instructions on how to form the shapes. This is quite difficult; recording constructions with a video camera is a good short-cut for remembering string figures, but video tends to collapse three-dimensional shapes into two dimensions, which makes string figures difficult to reconstruct.

- Older students may be asked to do more complex reasoning and constructions: for example, make a quadrilateral with two opposite angles equal and the other two unequal; transform it smoothly into a right triangle.

9-9. Further Activities

Shape jam. This exciting game leads students quickly to complex irregular three-dimensional figures. Work in groups of four people. Each group gets one loop of string. First one person holds the loop taut at two points (some of the string may dangle). Then the second person grabs the loop at two more points, possibly unhooking parts of the string held by the first person. The third person enters and grabs the loop at two more points, and so on. Once all group members are holding the loop, the first person lets go and grabs the loop at two new points, the second person lets go and grabs the loop at two new points, and so on. Try making shapes in which parts of the string loop around other parts to create extra corners in space.

Symmetry jam. Students work in pairs. Each student has a loop of string. One student leads, the other follows in rotational symmetry (see exercises in chapter 6 *Watch Your p's and q's*). See what shapes they can make. As part of the movements they can link their strings, or exchange who is holding which parts of which strings. Even if they move symmetrically they will find that the string figures will sometimes become asymmetrical.

Many loops. What shapes can a small group make if every person in the group has a loop of string? Try working with different colored strings. Create dances in which dancers make many individual shapes that relate to each other in space. One performer may sometimes hold parts of more than one loop.

Rope dances. Research uses of ropes and ribbons in dance and physical performance. For instance, cowboys do tricks with lassos, and rhythmic gymnasts draw patterns in the air with ribbons. Modern dance choreographer Alwin Nikolais' dance "Tensile Involvement," uses huge elastic bands that not only create shapes as big as the stage, but even extend into the wings.

Bigger loops. In one of our stage performances we used rope that is thicker and a bit longer than the string used in this chapter. Loops should be large enough for them to make a rectangles held by outstretched hands and feet; the total length of rope should be almost three times body height. Our big loops require about 15 feet of rope. We prefer one-inch thick cotton rope, which shows up well at a distance. One-inch thick rope is heavy and expensive, however — our arms hurt during rehearsal until we build up strength! To avoid straining muscles, use 1/2-inch cotton or nylon rope.
- Have students play with the large loops. They should begin slowly. Ask them how it feels to be enclosed in the loop of string. Can they travel while inside the string? Watch what students are doing and bring different approaches to the class's attention, so they see some of the movement possibilities.
- Ask students, "Which of the shapes that we made with small loops can be made using large loops? Since you are making these shapes by yourself, how will you have to use your legs or your head?"
- Which of the shapes above can one person make with such a loop? Which can two people make? (The tetrahedron may be difficult, but not impossible, for one person to construct.)
- Have each student create a sequence of shapes, along with transitions from shape to shape. Demonstrate the sequences to the class. Add music (see suggestions in chapter 13) and have several students perform their phrases at the same time.
- Have students work in small groups to create combined phrases. One way to do this is to have students teach each other their own phrases, and then have the group work on how to combine the elements that they like in each.
- Dances which combine several loops and several dancers can become complex quickly. Advise the students to work simply and try to repeat their discoveries often so as not to lose them.

Room-sized loops.

For giant string figures which involve two or three performers, we use loops that require as much as 60 to 80 feet of rope. Of course these figures require a very large space in which to perform. For classroom work we recommend 1/2-inch nylon rope, with about 50 feet of rope per loop.

- **Tangle/Untangle.** Work one big loop, about 60 feet in circumference. Each person in class holds the loop at one point. Have everyone move around, tangling the loop. Then untangle it, without talking.
- **Giant string figures.** Learn to make a traditional string figure with your hands. Can you learn to make a large version of the same figure using a giant loop of rope and two people in place of hands? Not all string figures work this way, but a surprisingly large number do. This exercise is related to chapters 11 and 12, *Giant Tangrams*.

Storytelling. Traditional string figures were often used to accompany storytelling. Have students learn traditional string figures, and use them and the geometric figures in this section to tell their own stories. (See the references for books on traditional string figures.) Try using string of different colors (cotton string may be died with fabric dye; nylon string will also take dye, though not as well). Several students might alternate making figures so that the audience mostly sees the result, not the construction of the figures. The students might choreograph simple movement so that they are moving, telling the story verbally, and making the figures, all the same time. We tell such string stories in some of our math dance performances. The dancers we work with always say this is much harder to learn than any of the other dances, since it involves speaking while moving, and doing small manipulations with fingers that are not part of usual dance training.

The Platonic solids. Find other ways to make the tetrahedron, octahedron and cube. Try making the other two regular polyhedra (also called Platonic solids) — the dodecahedron (12 pentagonal faces) and icosahedron (20 triangular faces). How many people will you need to make each figure? What is the simplest method for making each of these figures? Can you transform one shape to another moving through all five Platonic solids? To get you started, here are some other ways to transform loops of string into polyhedra. You will have to figure out which hand goes where (but RH means Right Hand, etc.)

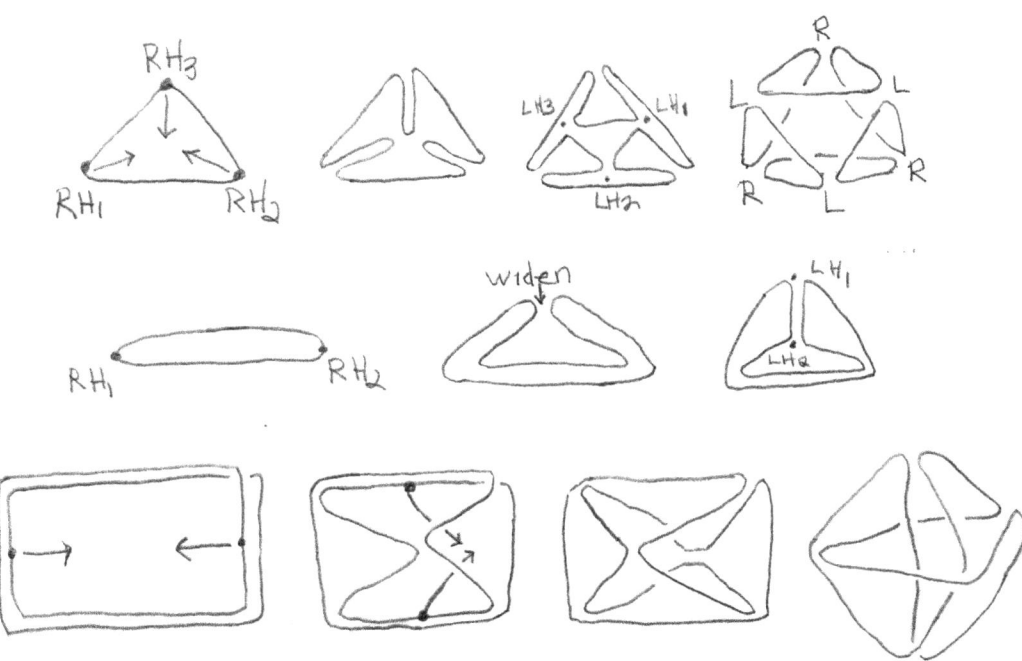

9-10. Resources

Coxeter, H. S. M. *Regular Polytopes,* 3rd Ed. New York: Dover Publications, 1963,1973. A compendium of properties of polyhedra by the twentieth century's greatest geometer.

Fuse, Tomoko. *Unit Origami: Multidimensional Transformations.* Tokyo and New York: Japan Publications, Inc., 1990. Modular and polyhedral origami by the master of the form.

Gryski, Camilla, illustrated by Tom Sankey. *Cat's Cradle, Owl's Eyes: A Book of String Games* (1983), *Super String Games* (1987), New York: Beech Tree Books. *Many Stars and More String Games.* New York: William Morrow and Company, 1985. Very accessible collections of many figures from around the world, with clear instructions and beautiful illustrations.

George Hart's Pavilion of Polyhedreality. An elaborate online art gallery of polyhedron models, with references to books and other web sites. http://euch3i.chem.emory.edu/proposal/www.li.net/~george/pavilion.html. Also see Vladimir Bulatov's polyhedron gallery at http://www.physics.orst.edu/~bulatov/polyhedra/.

Hart, George W., and Henri Picciotto. *Zome Geometry: Hands-on Learning with Zome (TM) Models.* Emeryville, CA: Key Curriculum Press, 2001. Classroom explorations with polyhedra, utilizing the Zometools models.

Hilton, Peter, and Jean Pederson. *Build Your Own Polyhedra.* Menlo Park, CA: Addison Wesley Publishing Company, 1994. Intriguing and enjoyable mathematical recreations with polyhedra that involve building them with various materials, and the theory that goes with it.

International String Figure Association. *Bulletin of the International String Figure Association* (annual), *String Figure Magazine* (quarterly). http://www.isfa.org, Pasadena, California. See their online bibliography, as well as links to many other sites. They publish an academic journal (the Bulletin), and an accessible popular magazine (*String Figure Magazine*).

Jayne, Caroline Furness. *String Figures and How to make Them: A Study of Cat's Cradle in Many Lands.* New York: Dover Publications, 1906 and 1962. The classic collection of over 100 string figures.

Lawson, Joan. *A Ballet-maker's Handbook: Sources, Vocabulary, Styles.* New York: Theatre Arts Books/Routledge, 1991. Cover photo from Ashton's "Fille mal Gardee," shows dancers with collapsed tetrahedral shape made with length of fabric.

Senechal, Marjorie, and George Fleck, editors. *Shaping Space: A Polyhedral Approach.* Boston: Birkhauser, 1988. Inspired by a conference in 1984, contains diverse group of articles on polyhedra.

Stewart, Ian. "Dances with Dodecahedra," in *Scientific American,* Sep. 1999, volume 281, Number 3. Short article about Karl Schaffer and Scott Kim's dances with polyhedral string figures.

Walker, Jearl. Cat's cradles and other topologies formed with a two-meter loop of flexible string," in The Amateur Scientist, *Scientific American,* 1985, 252(5): 138-143. Essay on the mathematical ideas in cat's cradle.

9-11. Handout for *Figures in String*

Try making these figures with four people and a single loop of string. Which figures can be made without doubling the string along any of the edges? Can you smoothly transform one shape into another? What other shapes can you make?

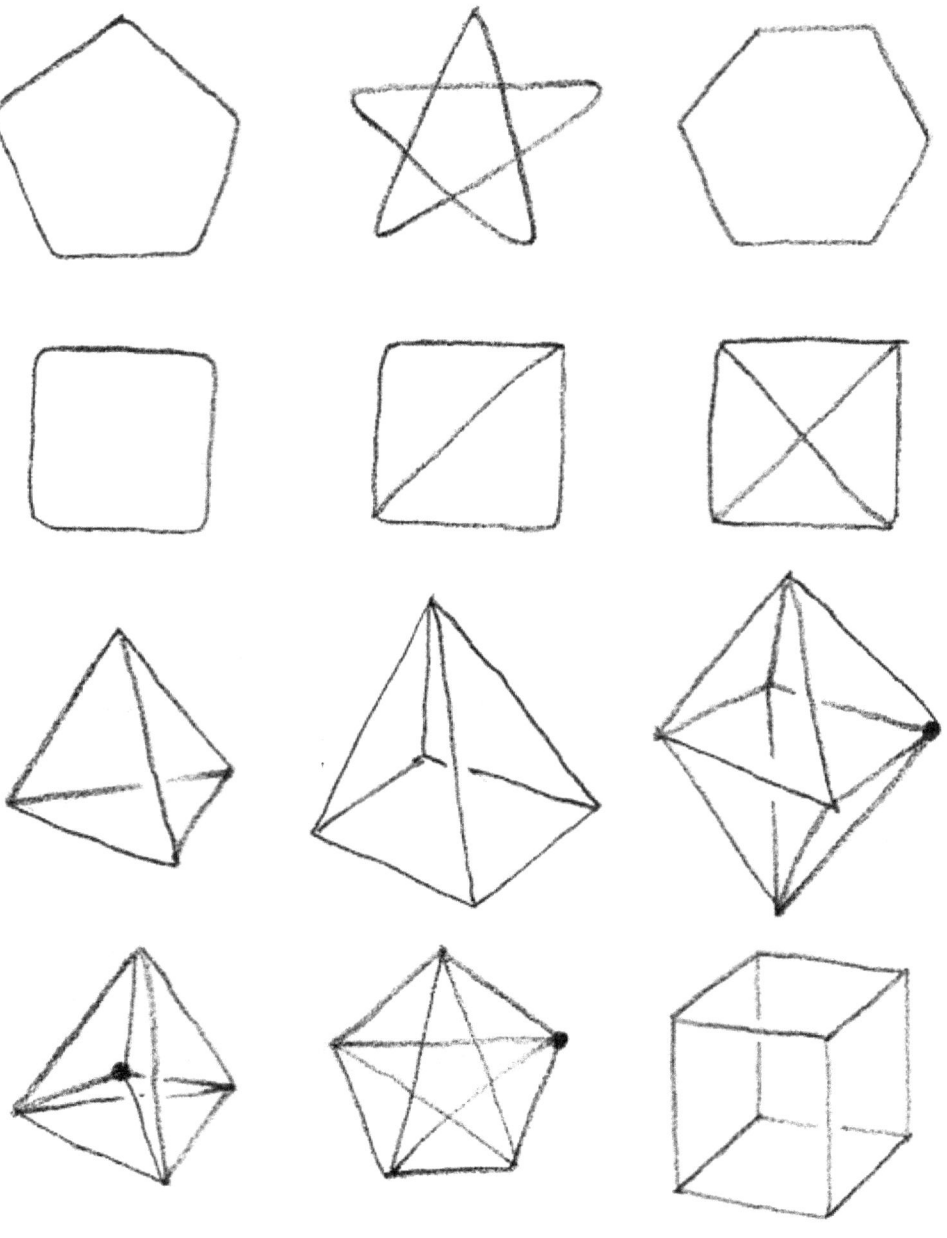

Math Dance with Dr. Schaffer and Mr. Stern • © 2001 Schaffer, Stern, Kim • www.mathdance.org

CHAPTER 10
Stick Figures
Making large forms in space

Grades:	5–12
Time:	30-60 minutes
Groups of:	Solo, then groups of 2- 6
Concepts:	Polyhedra, moving as a group (ensemble), and handling props as an extension of the body
Materials:	Each participant needs a pair of PVC pipes tied together by string at one end. See instructions at the end of this chapter for making "Geometry Sticks."
Space:	Large high open space, like a gym or outdoors
Related activities:	Chapter 9 *String Figures* (similar issues, different materials)
	Chapters 5, 6, 7 (*Threesies, Watch Your p's and q's, Twisted Addition*)

In this chapter groups of students make shapes using geometry sticks — forty inch long white PVC plastic pipes. When we first had students use the geometry sticks, it became apparent that the size of the props demands use of the whole body and close attention to safety. Moreover, making group shapes requires cooperation and a sense of unity in the group. The "outside eye" is strengthened because dancers must picture what they are doing in relation to the overall group shape as well as to the individual members nearby.

The mathematics is made very visible and the all members of the group must understand the overall shape. The bright whiteness of PVC pipe places more attention on the motion of the sticks than on the performers. However, as the work progresses, encourage students to notice how the participants' movements affect the way the dance looks. Attention to these aspects of movement enhances the dancing.

We have choreographed a number of dances using PVC pipes, both for our dance company and for dance students. In the pictures below, Gregg Lizenbery joins Karl and Erik in "Shadowed Flight."

Dance Note: Props in Dance
Dance traditions throughout the world use props. These include, for example, the Russian Folk dance "Dance of the Sabres," the Navaho "Hoop Dance," and the use of skirts in Mexican Folklorica. Modern dance choreographers have long been fascinated with props: Alwin Nikolais used long elastic ropes in "Tensile Involvement", and Martha Graham used a tube of stretchy fabric in "Lamentation." The popular rhythmic group Stomp exploits the visual and aural possibilities of everything from bic lighters to trash cans. Some martial artists and dancers are familiar with moving with poles. One variety of Philippine stick dance involves pairs of kneeling dancers performing rhythmic patterns on the floor with sticks while dancers move their feet between and the around the sticks.

10-1. Try this (5-10 minutes)

Before you give students the props, discuss the potential hazards (the sticks might hit the eyes, for example). Make certain the students always pay attention to the sticks and where they are moving them. Tell students, "At the beginning, do not move the sticks unless you are looking at them." Later, when they are more comfortable with the props, they can learn to sense where the sticks are.

The goal of these warm-up exercises is to move clearly and smoothly with the props. Try a few of the following exercises until students get the hang of moving gracefully without bumping into anyone else. Remember, moving slowly is the key to safety! Have the students:

- Spread throughout the room.
- Watch the sticks as they move them very slowly. Move one stick slowly in a floating motion and keep the other still, then reverse. Move both sticks slowly. What kind of motions are easier to do?
- Move the sticks down, up, left, right, then repeat. Raise as high as is comfortable; down as low as is comfortable.
- Move their bodies while keeping the sticks still. Keep their bodies relatively still while moving the sticks.
- Attach one end of the stick to the end of another person's stick. Then let the ends float apart. Repeat.
- Make a right angle. Make an angle half that size. Choose an angle to make, then move it through space without altering the angle.
- Make up their own variations.

10-2. Moving in Pairs (5-10 minutes)

In these exercises students learn to make specific geometric shapes and to improvise forms with no specific model in mind. Freezing — holding the sticks still — is key. It is easy either to let the sticks float or to not hold a shape with energy. Remind students, "Be clear about when you are moving and when you are still!" Once students are comfortable with an exercise, encourage them to allow everyone to see the shapes by not blocking the geometry sticks. "Be aware not only of the sticks' shape, but the complete shape made with your bodies and the sticks."

- **Shape-shift**. Students pair up. First person in the pair makes a shape and freezes. Second person adds on to that shape and freezes, while the first person moves to new shape. Repeat. The sticks may or may not be touching. They may be or may not be in the same plane. The shapes do not have to resemble recognizable geometric forms — just play!
- **Two-person square**. Each pair makes a square, and fluidly flexes it to make a non-square rhombus. Have students grasp the ends of the two stick segments which are not attached by string; this makes the shape more stable. Have students make a 4-sided figure which is not a rhombus,
- **Spell your name**. Each pair chooses one name and spells it letter by letter with the pipes. Have them practice until they are able to move fluidly from one letter to the next. Have several pairs demonstrate their names. If everyone already knows everybody else's name (as in a class rather than a workshop), have them make up a name and see if the rest of the class can understand what they have spelled.

10-3. Moving in Groups (10-15 minutes)

In this activity, shape-shift (see section 9-2) is expanded to three, four or five participants. Keep in mind that larger groups require more self-discipline with this exercise and must hold the shapes longer.
- Number the members of your group. Number one makes a shape with her pipes and freezes. Number two adds his pipes to make a shape involving four pipes and freezes. Number three adds her pipes to the growing shape and freezes. Now two and three freeze while number one moves her sticks to form another shape. Continue in this manner, improvising new shapes.
- Suggestions for students: "Fullfill the shapes. Once you feel comfortable with shape-shift, pay attention to how your bodies are moving as well. Can you vary the speed of the shape-shift? If your group habitually makes one kind of shape, what can you do to change that?"

Shape-shift can be taken in many directions:
- Split the class into two groups which take turns watching each other in shape-shift. Have the students discuss what they see.
- Each group re-creates three shapes they really liked from the shape-shift improvisation (or they can make up fun shapes that were not part of the improvisation). The group chooses an order for the three shapes. They practice the sequence and perform to music. When making dances, recognizable geometric forms are also fair game.
- Have students use their sequences of three shapes to tell a story, demonstrate a geometric idea, or address both a story and a geometric idea at the same time.
- (Note: Some of the most interesting choreography arises from transitions. which are how the group moves between shapes. Make a list with the class of possible approaches to transitions. Two such examples we have seen students use are: 1) float apart, and 2) break apart percussively in succession.)

10-4. Polyhedra (10-15 minutes)

In this activity, students work in groups of three or six to create two and three-dimensional forms.
- In groups of three, have students make a tetrahedron (a pyramid with a triangular base.) Ask them, "Can you construct it and hold it so that it doesn't rest on the floor?" They may want to hold the joints where sticks meet. Have students practice moving their shape so that the tetrahedron does not fall apart, but moves slowly and continuously. Have students practice making the tetrahedron shape and then pulling the geometry sticks apart slowly.
- In groups of three, have student make a hexagon. Ask students, "Can you flex it, without breaking it apart at the joints, so that it folds into a tetrahedron? If not, why not?
- In groups of six, have students make a cube. As with the tetrahedron, it is more challenging to make it so it is not resting on the floor, and each group should practice moving it through space. Have students practice forming and unforming the cube shape. Ask students: "Can you rotate the cube to demonstrate its axes of three-fold symmetry? Its axes of two-fold symmetry? Can you flex it to form a hexagonal shape? A 4-pointed star?"
- In groups of six, have students make an octahedron, following similar rules as with the tetrahedron and cube. Can the octahedron be flexed without it falling apart? How is it thus different from the cube?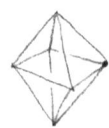

10-5. Expanding The Dance

- Once students have sketched out a movement sequence, encourage them to practice silently. Adding music, besides making the dance more interesting, encourages students to feel the movement they are doing rather than chat distractedly while performing.
- Discuss with the class the form of the shape sequences: How do the shapes within a particular sequence relate? How do they differ?
- Discuss beginnings and endings: Do the dancers begin on stage, or enter the space? Do dancers end on stage, or should they exit?
- Ask students "What is the quality of motion of each sequence of shapes?" Have them explore how a quality of motion can be performed better (e.g. if the sticks are supposed to float into a shape, how can the bodies also float? Shifting weight from one foot to another smoothly is quite tricky. How does one improve that?).
- As a class, take all the group movement sequences and place them in an order. Try to create an entire dance out of what results.
- Have students discuss how the sequences make the audience feel, what they liked best, what they didn't like, and ways to improve.
- Discuss some of the difficulties of handling the props, and some of the solutions that students came up with. Are there particular approaches that all agree on?

10-6. Reflection & Assessment

The Dance

Assessing the dance.
- Did groups work together? Did they try the exercises?
- Did they freeze well? Did they fulfill their shapes?
- Were they able to demonstrate their sequence of shapes? Did the clarity of the presentation improve with practice?
- Did students explore the transitions between shapes?
- Did the clarity of movement of the body as it relates to the props improve as they practiced?
- Videotape students and have them critique their own work.

Questions for discussion
- What props have you seen dancers perform with?
- What other props could you use besides poles to form shapes in space in performance?
- How could you make the performers vanish visually so the pipes would appear to dance in space by themselves?

The Mathematics

Assessing the mathematics.
- Did students correctly assemble the geometric shapes (square, tetrahedron, etc.)?
- Did all members of the groups participate in assembling the shapes?
- Did they improve at coordinating as a group as they progressed?
- Have the class draw the shapes they made in their groups, paying attention to perspective.

Questions for discussion.
- Have the students picture a particular geometric shape from this exercise in their minds, then ask them questions about that shape: "How many edges or segments does it have? How many faces or polygons? How many points or vertices? How many segments join at each point? What are the sizes of the angles? Are all the angles the same?" If they have difficulties answering the questions, have them reconstruct the shapes and look for the answers in the shapes, or consult their pictures or models.
- When making the tetrahedron in groups of three, is it possible to do so in such a way that there is no vertex where three ends of sticks come together (these are difficult-to-hold vertices)? Why or why not? (Answer: there are a total of four vertices in the tetrahedron, but only three joints where stick-ends are joined by string, so there must be exactly one such vertex).
- The tetrahedron and the hexagon both have the same number of edges or sticks: six. So why does it seem to be impossible to deform the hexagon until it looks like the tetrahedron? (One answer: think about the vertex in the previous question which has three unjoined stick ends — if it were possible to so deform the hexagon, such a vertex could exist only by breaking apart the loop of the hexagon.)
- How many sticks come together at each vertex of the cube? Is it possible for six people to make the cube without any vertices where three unjoined sticks come together? Why or why not?
- How many sticks come together at each vertex of the octahedron? Is it possible for six performers to make the octahedron so that there are no vertices where four unjoined sticks come together? If so, how? (Note: this is not only possible, it is mandatory; each of the six vertices must have exactly one string-joint.)
- Advanced topic: Euler circuits. Discuss with the class what an Euler circuit is (see *String Figures*, Chapter 9). Then ask: "Do either the cube or octahedron have Euler circuits?" This problem shows that constructing such an Euler circuit "backwards" by flexing the circuit into the polyhedron's skeleton is somewhat more difficult than tracing over the figure of the skeleton without lifting the pencil.

10-7. Further Activities

Dodecagon. Ask the class to make a dodecagon (12-sided figure) by joining or connecting six pairs of geometry sticks with string. "Can it be flexed without falling apart to form a cube? An octahedron? If not, explain why it cannot be done. If it can, do it!" This figure is more easily manipulated and many new mathematical and movement problems are suggested. For example: "How many triangles can you make? Can you make four squares? Can you make an animal that moves? A sequence of shapes that flow one to the other?"

Three-pipe units. Connect three pipes end-to-end. How does this change the movement properties? Does it change the shapes that can be made? (With these, two people can make a tetrahedron, or four people can make a cube or octahedron, in a variety of ways.)

Other pipe combinations. Connect four pipes together in a square. Each student gets one square. Explore moving with these units. Choose two different lengths of pipe and combine them. Invent a different way to connect the pipes.

10-8. Resources

Check out the dances of Alwin Nikolais, who often used props in creative ways.
Find a video of Martha Graham's solo "Lamentation," in which she used a costume as both prop and cloak.
Investigate the work of juggler Michael Moschen. See the reference at the end of chapter 8.
Read about Buckminster Fuller's movable models of the "Jitterbug" (the cuboctahedron).

10-9. How to Make the "Geometry Sticks"

We use "schedule 125" pipe (the thinner pipe), 3/4" in diameter, and 40" in length for older students (grades 7 through adult, shorter for younger children. We use 1" diameter for our performances.) The pipe is inexpensive and available at most hardware stores. It can easily be cut with a circular saw or a special PVC pipe cutter which is often available at hardware stores for the customers' use. We drilled a hole in one end of each pipe section, and joined them with thin clothes line rope. We also put a piece of contact tape over each end, to prevent any accidents with the sometimes sharp end edges. You can sand the edges if they are jagged.

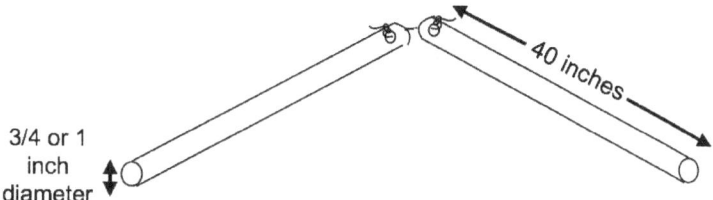

If you don't have enough to go around, have students take turns. The students waiting can try to make the shapes with their arms or legs!

CHAPTER 11
Moving with Giant Tangrams
Making geometric shapes dance in space

Grades:	3–12
Time:	20–60 minutes
Math Concepts:	Shape, angle, area
Dance Concepts:	Dance with props, spatial relations
Group size:	4-7
Space:	Requires clear floor
Materials:	One large tangram set per group (see instructions on page 109).
	Optional: pencil and paper, small tangram sets, ruler
Prerequisites:	None
Related Activities:	Chapter 11 *Moving with Giant Tangrams* (follow-on activity)
	Chapter 10 *Stick Figures* (also involves moving with large props)

Tangrams, a geometric puzzle invented in China over 200 years ago, is played by millions of people all over the world, making it one of the most popular puzzles of all time. The goal of tangrams is to arrange seven simple shapes — a square, parallelogram and five triangles — to make silhouettes of animals, people, and other familiar figures. In the early 1800s a woman in China named Shu Fen Shih wrote a book containing over 1700 different figures. In the 1900s the great American puzzle inventor Sam Loyd created a gallery of 300 tangram faces, many of which are recognizable as particular people. Nowadays tangrams are a common classroom manipulative in elementary schools for teaching geometry and art.

In this chapter you will read about movement games with giant tangram pieces a foot or two in size, starting with solo exercises and working toward group exercises. By moving tangrams in space students develop their spatial visualization abilities and become acutely aware of geometric relationships. The activities in this chapter can be used on their own, or as preparation for the next chapter, *Storytelling with Giant Tangrams*.

Although a few of these activities are similar to exercises with conventional small tangrams, giant tangrams have several unique advantages. Giant tangrams require cooperation since one person cannot hold all the pieces. Because pieces can be seen across the room they lead naturally to performance and storytelling. The spatial visualization challenges are harder since you cannot see the shape you are making. Finally forming shapes with a group requires working out complex logistics among several people.

Many forms of dance from around the world use props, from Russian sword dances to Native American hoop dances. Acrobatic groups like Cirque du Soleil use props like giant balls as part of precarious balancing acts. Modern dance groups like the Alwin Nikolais Dance Theater create dances of brightly colored shapes by hiding the performers in black costumes against a black background.

11–1 Moving Individually (5-10 minutes)

Before beginning, make several sets of giant tangrams. At a minimum make enough so each student has one piece. For instructions, see section 11-9.

In this activity, students learn to move giant tangram pieces that are a foot or two in size. It is not necessary to do every exercise, just enough so students feel comfortable with the prop.

- Clear the space by pushing desks to the side of your classroom. Or move the class to a gym or other large space. Give each person one tangram piece. Have students stand in two lines facing each other, so they can see each other's shapes more clearly.
- For each of the following directions, have half the class move while the other half watches, then switch, so everyone gets to move and watch. After each exercise ask students to talk about what they saw that did or did not work well. For instance, slow controlled motion is usually clearer than fast careless motion. Seeing what works when other people move is a good way to improve your own movement — see the note on critiquing movement below.
- Explore the space. "Hold your shape in one hand, move it around slowly without moving your feet. Raise it as high as you can, as low as you can, in front of your neighbor to the left, and to the right."
- Change the angle. "Twirl your shape by the handle. Turn it so it is as narrow as possible from left to right. Turn it so it as wide as possible."
- Explore different movement qualities. "Move it slowly and smoothly. Move it staccatto, in sudden movements with long pauses in between. Move the piece as if it were heavy and hard to move. Move it as if it were light as a feather."
- Keep it flat. "Try moving it so the front face stays flat in a plane, as if you were washing a big window, with the handle side toward you. This is how you usually want to hold the tangrams when you are performing for an audience, because the shapes are clearest."
- Keep it still. "Try keeping the shape still in space as if were glued to a pole while you move around, under and over it. How still can you hold the shape?"
- "Use your voice to add sound effects as you move your tangram pieces. What sounds work best with what movements?" W often encourage students to add sound effects to all the tangram exercises in this chapter. In the next chapter students add narration to their tangram movements.

Dance Note: Critique

Learning to look at dance is a big part of learning to move. When one is performing a dance, it is difficult to really see it, so it is important to get other people to say what they see. Encouraging students to talk about their responses helps them become aware of their reactions, learn from each other, and develop an eye for dance. Critiquing the work is a part of all the arts — visual art, music, writing — but is especially important in dance and theater where the performers are part of the art itself.

What sorts of comments do we want students to give? We are not interested in whether a particular movement conforms to a particular performance technique like an arabesque in ballet or a step-ball-change in jazz. All ways of moving are welcome.

Instead, we are interested in which movements work best for the students as they watch the dances. Ask the students: "What ways of moving seem interesting? What catches your attention? What surprises you? What do you find distracting? What new ideas do you see that you might want to add to your own dances?" Avoid personal remarks; comment on movement, not people. Sometimes it is fine to ask students to say what they liked, other times it is better to ask them to say what worked for them.

Of course students may have different opinions about what is interesting. That is okay. The overall goal of critiquing dance should be for the class as a whole to build up a collective understanding of what types of movement work best.

As a teacher, also look for whether students move with clarity and authority. Whatever they are doing, are they doing it fully, with complete commitment? Often it is better not to suggest ways to fix problems, but merely to point them out. For more about critiquing dance, see chapter 14, *Assessment*.

11–2 Moving in Pairs (5–10 minutes)

Try this exercise with half of each group moving and half watching. The "movers" do the following:
- "Find a partner and stand side by side. Hold your pieces in front of you facing the audience, keeping them completely still."
- "One of you slowly move your piece until it joins the other person's piece to make a shape. Now the first person holds their piece still, while the second person slowly moves their piece until it joins to make a different shape. Take turns moving the pieces to make different shapes. Only one person should move at a time."
- "Now try moving your pieces at the same time, always keeping them in contact with each other. Move slowly so you don't lose contact."
- Optional: "Join with another pair of people to make a group of four. See if you can move all four pieces at the same time, always keeping pieces in contact with each other."

After the movers have finished moving, the "watchers" critique the motions by considering some the following questions. There are no right and wrong answers to these questions, but the act of answering these questions will help everyone see what is going on.
- "What did you notice when the other group moved?"
- "For each type of movement, what worked? What did not work?"
- "What are the different ways you saw that people moved from one shape to another?"
- "What did you like or not like about the way pieces came into contact?"
- "How could you do it better? How could you do it differently?"
- "What feelings or images did different types of movement call to mind?"
- "What type of music would be appropriate for each type of movement?"
- "What other things move that way?"

11–3 Moving in Groups (5–10 minutes)

Divide students into groups of seven, each group holding a complete tangram set. If there are too few people in a group, some people can hold more than one piece. For children ages eight and under, use fewer pieces and smaller groups.
- "Make a shape with all pieces in your group. Try not to stand in front of your tangrams, so the audience can see the shapes."
- "Make the widest shape you can. The tallest. The most compact."
- "Make a shape with a hole in it."
- "Make a square using some or all the pieces."
- "Can you bring all your shapes together at a point so they completely fill 360° around the point, with leaving any gaps?"
- "Make a shape. Now make the mirror image of the shape. Does the parallelogram get in the way? How"

11–4 Shape-Shift (5–10 minutes)

This group improvisation often generates wonderful and unusual tangram forms. Have half the class perform while the other half sits and watches, then do the opposite, so everyone gets a chance to watch. Forms usually look best if shapes all face the audience with handles in back and everyone behind the tangrams, though sometimes the handles should be in front or the pieces might be at a different angle.
- One person in each group holds up a piece, keeping it still.
- A second person joins a piece to touch the first piece, and so on, until all the pieces are part of one big shape.
- Now everyone holds their pieces still, except the first person, who moves a piece to join the other pieces at a different place.
- Then the second person moves a piece to a new place, and so on.

11–5 Coordinated Movements (5–10 minutes)

This movement activity develops a sense of ensemble.
- Work in pairs. Each person holds one piece.
- Explore how the two pieces can move in relation to each other. Hold one piece still while the other moves. Try moving both at the same time. Have both pieces move with the same movement quality or different movement qualities. Move pieces in unison or in opposition. Have one piece bump into the other, causing it to move. Pretend both pieces are part of a larger machine.
- Choose three of these coordinated motions and perform them in sequence.
- Try the same activity with groups of three people.

11-6. Reflections and Assessment

The Dance
The essential movement problem in this chapter is the same as in puppetry: to breathe life into an inanimate object. Here are ways to develop the dance aspects of moving with tangrams.
- **Slow down.** The most important thing to know about moving with tangrams is that slow, controlled movements generally work better than fast, chaotic motions, because slow movements draw the eye to the props. Of course quicker movements are still useful as punctuation.
- **Space hold.** To create the illusion that tangram pieces are floating in space, have students practice a "space hold." divide students into groups of three. Each group works with just one tangram piece. First one person holds the piece still in space while the other two people move around it. Then a second person takes over holding the piece still in space while the other two people move around it. Then the third person takes over holding the piece. Continue taking turns having one person hold the piece while the other two move around it, making sure the piece never moves. Beware of moving the piece during handoffs, or when the person holding the piece moves.
- **Turning.** Turn a piece so it appears to rotate around one of its corners, not around the handle. Stop moving, then resume turning, this time around another corner. It takes concentration to do this well.
- **No fidgeting.** Encourage students to eliminate extraneous movements and fidgeting that draw attention away from the shapes — unless they are using their bodies as parts of the shapes. A good way to have students refine the way they move is to have them perform a tangram dance in pantomime without the pieces. This requires good spatial memory.

- **Qualities of motion**. A single shape can convey many different moods depending on how it moves. Choose three adverbs such as happily, slyly, and confusedly, and have students move their pieces in each of these ways. Be sure to consider fast and slow, standing still or moving through space, high and low. Put the three moods in sequence and perform them for the rest of the group.
- **Movies**. Since the invention of film, animators have created movies that are pure dances of shapes in space. View sequences from Walt Disney's Fantasia, the films of Norman McLaren, or the films of Oskar Fischinger. What can be used from these movies in the tangram dances?
- **Beginning and end**. Any of the activities in this chapter can be developed further into a complete dance by asking the questions: How does it begin? How does it develop? How does it end?

The Mathematics

There are many books of mathematical activities with small tangrams. Here are some mathematical group activities that work particularly well with giant tangrams. These activities work best if each group has a complete set of seven tangram pieces. If there are fewer than seven people in a group, one person can hold more than one piece. Younger students may want to work in smaller groups with fewer pieces, since younger children are more comfortable performing for the one or two other people in their group than for an entire audience.

- **Noticing shapes**. "Look at all the shapes in your group. Which pieces have the same shape? Which pieces have the same shape, but are different sizes? What is each shape called? How many sides does each piece have? What is the smallest angle on your shape? The biggest angle? The shortest side? The longest side? Which piece has the biggest angle?"
- **Lengths**. Divide students into groups of 4 to 7. "Some tangram pieces have edges that are exactly the same length. Move your piece so it joins someone else's piece along two edges that exactly match. Can you join all the pieces in your group into one big shape so pieces meet only along edges that exactly match? Can you find another way to do it?"
- **Angles**. Divide students into groups of 4 to 7. "Split your group into two groups. One group bring your pieces together at a point to make an angle. The other group see if you can bring your pieces together at a point to make the same angle. Then trade which group makes the angle and which group copies it. How many different angles can you make using any number of pieces in your group? Can you bring pieces together at a point so they completely fill up 360° without leaving a gap? What is the fewest number of pieces that can do this?"
- **Areas**. Divide students into groups of 4 to 7. "Which shapes can be made of other shapes? How many of the smallest triangle would you need to make each of the other shapes? Make two shapes that are identical."
- **Drawing**. "Record shapes you held in the air. You can draw on paper or work with small tangram pieces. Plan shapes small on paper, then see if you can make them big in the air." Like Chapter 4, *Spatial Paths*, this activity exercises spatial visualization skills, translating between small and large, the difference between horizontal and vertical, and solo and group work.

11-7. Further Activities

Here are further movement activities that use tangrams and other large shapes.

Shapes in the Room. Everyone holds one tangram piece. "Position your piece in relation to a shape you see in the room, such as a corner of a chair, an edge of a table, or a pattern on the floor. Move your piece so it reinforces the shapes you see. Feel free to interact with other tangram pieces, as well as shapes in the room."

Machine. This is a variation of a popular theatrical improvisation exercise. Divide students into groups of 4 to 7, with one piece per person. One person in each group starts moving a piece in a motion that repeats after about two or three seconds. Vocal sound effects should be encouraged. For instance the piece might suddenly move to the right, then slowly move back to the left. After a few repetitions a second person joins the machine by adding a second moving piece that interacts with the first piece in a repeating motion. One by one all the people in the group join the machine, making a complex repeating motion. Once everyone has joined the machine, gradually speed up the machine until it falls apart. Build several machines and have them all interact.

Animation. Another way to make shapes dance in space is to animate them. Get a digital video camera that can record one frame at a time, mount it on a tripod, and point it down at a table. Arrange tangram pieces on the table, record one frame, move the pieces a little, record another frame, and so on. Another way to make an animated movie is to use an animation program such as Flash. Draw the seven tangram pieces in Flash, assigning each piece to a different layer. Arrange the pieces in a shape on one key frame, then arrange the shapes differently on a second key frame. Animate the pieces by using "inbetweening" to make them move smoothly from one key frame to the next.

Math note: Dissection

The seven tangram pieces can be cut out of a square. Mathematicians call cutting a shape into smaller shapes "dissection." Note that every tangram piece can be dissected into one, two or four identical isosceles right triangles:

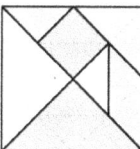

Dissection is useful for showing that two shapes have the same area. For instance, we can use dissection to show that a parallelogram and a rectangle with the same base and height have equal areas, as shown below.

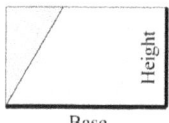 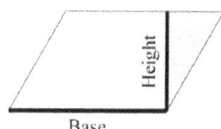

Similarly, we can dissect a triangle to show it has half the area of a rectangle with the same base and height.

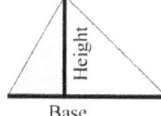 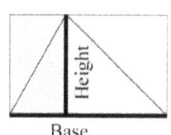

We can prove the Pythagorean theorem by dissecting the large square below in two different ways. Notice that the two white squares on the sides of the gray right triangle in the diagram on the left must have the same area as the larger white square on the hypotenuse of the same gray triangle in the diagram on the right. This method is based on an ancient Chinese proof of the Pythagorean theorem prior to the sixth century BC – that predates Pythagoras! (Note: the theorem says that $a^2 + b^2 = c^2$.)

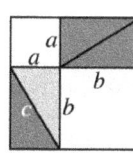 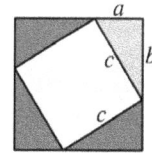

Mathematicians have proved that any two shapes with the same area bounded by straight edges can be dissected into one another. The key is to realize that any polygonal shape can be cut into triangles, and any triangle can be dissected into a rectangle.

11-8. Resources

Educational Design. Large Tangram. Includes 70 design cards.

ETA/Cuisenare. Tangram Kit. Mathematical classroom activities using tangrams, including two sets of plastic tangram pieces and 20 activity cards.

Frederickson, Greg N. *Dissections: Plane & Fancy*. Cambridge University Press, 1997. The best book on the mathematics of dissections. Fascinating, sophisticated yet accessible, with many pictures.

Gardner, Martin. "More on Tangrams." Article originally published in Scientific American, Sep 1974, anthologized in Time Travel and Other Mathematical Bewilderments by Martin Gardner, W. H. Freeman and Company, 1988. Discusses more advanced mathematical problems like forming "snug" or convex figures.

Han, S. T. Tangram software. http://hometown.aol.com/sth777/page0.html. An excellent tangram program popular in schools. For Macintosh or Windows.

Iota Center. http://www.iotacenter.org. Nonprofit organization promoting abstract animated films. Includes traveling exhibitions, information on purchasing videos, and links to movies on the web. Look here for information on such abstract filmmakers as Norman McLaren and Oskar Fischinger.

Irvin, Barbara Bando. *Geometry and Fractions with Tangrams*. Learning Resources 1995. Over forty K-6 activities.

Loyd, Sam. *Sam Loyd's Book of Tangram Puzzles (The 8th Book of Tan Part I)*, Sam Loyd, Dover Publications, 1968. Hundreds of figures by the great American puzzle inventor.

Nelsen, Roger B. *Proofs without Words: Exercises in Visual Thinking*. The Mathematical Association of America, 1993. Marvelous visual proofs of theorems in geometry and number theory. In many cases a single diagram is the whole argument. Suitable for algebra and geometry students. Includes several dissection proofs of the Pythagorean theorem.

Read, Donald. *Tangrams, 330 Puzzles*. Dover Publications, 1965. Good source of tangram figures.

Rex Games. Tangoes. Commonly sold in toy stores. Includes figure cards, and two sets of pieces so two people can play at the same time.

Seymour, Dale. *Tangramath*, Creative Publications Inc., 1971. Reproducible activities that reinforce math concepts such as size, shape, congruence, similarity, properties of polygons, symmetry, and area. Solutions and supplemental open-ended activities are provided. Tangrams are required. Grades 1-10.

Walt Disney Pictures. *Fantasia 2000*. 75-minute film from. A collection of short animations in diverse visual styles set to works of classical music. The original Fantasia includes a purely abstract sequence of shapes moving to Bach's Toccata and Fugue in D Minor.

Yoshigahara, Nob. Shape by Shape. A toy published by Binary Arts. An interesting variation on tangrams with two colors of shapes that make both the positive and negative space of a picture. Includes 40 challenge cards.

11-9. How to Make Giant Tangrams

Here is a method for making a set of giant tangrams out of furniture foam. We have also seen tangram sets made of cardboard, styrofoam, foam core, spongy foam hot-glued to cardboard. Recently we have used 4' by 8' sections of rigid insulation styrofoam, which we cut on a table saw (see http://tinyurl.com/GiantTangramConstruction for details). Whatever method you use, keep in mind that the pieces will work best if they are made:

- Lightweight. If they drop, they will not hurt anyone.
- Thick edges. It is easier to have the edges meet if those edges are at least 2 inches thick.
- Centered handles. Centered handles make pieces easier to handle. It's better if the handles have knobs.
- Bright colors. Colors attract the eye, and help pieces stand out from the background.
- Big enough to see. For younger children, make the pieces smaller.

Shapes. Our favorite material is 2-inch thick poly foam, which is light, rigid, and soft enough that students will not hurt each other. 3-inch poly foam holds its shape better, but is heavier. Stores that sell furniture foam will often cut them for a nominal charge. Have them follow the plan shown on the next page. The assembled square is 32 inches on a side. A complete set costs about $20, including materials and labor. We do not recommend that readers cut pieces themselves, since stores do a better job than most people can do at home. Alternatively, use corrugated cardboard or foam core (available at art stores) instead of foam. Be sure edges are at least 2 inches thick, so it is easy to bring pieces together at an edge without missing.

Handles. Attaching handles is a bit tricky. Ask for help at a hardware store if not sure what to do. To get anything to stick to foam requires a lot of surface area, so we make our handles in two pieces: one to stick to the foam and one to hold with your hand. Cut out a 6-inch by 6-inch square of 1/8-inch thick masonite. Glue or screw a handle to the middle of the masonite square. Make handles out of a spool, a used 35mm film canister, a piece of dowel (1 inch diameter by 2 inches long), or a pop-up garden sprinkler head (a short section of plastic pipe can be screwed on and off the sprinkler head for compact storage). Handles work better if there is a knob at the end that prevents the hand from slipping off. Epoxy and/or screw a disk to the end of the dowel to make a knob.

Glue. Use spray adhesive to glue the masonite square with handle to the middle of each foam piece. Use epoxy glue to attach the handle to the masonite. Be sure to attach the handles at the center of gravity of each piece, so they balance or spin easily. Find the center of gravity of a tangram by finding the point where it can balance on one finger.

Decoration. Foam can be spray-painted, but be sure to use a series of light coats, letting each coat dry before applying the next coat. If foam is spray-painted all at once it may end up a soggy piece of foam that will never dry! Another method we like better is to cut a piece of felt a few inches larger than each foam piece, fold back the edges of each cloth piece to make a straight seam, then spray glue the cloth to the foam. Spray glue is unhealthy to breathe, so be sure to have good ventilation or work outside.

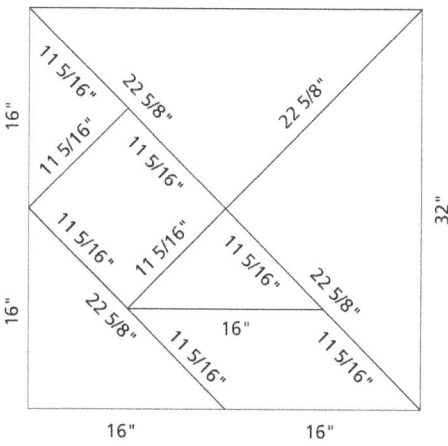
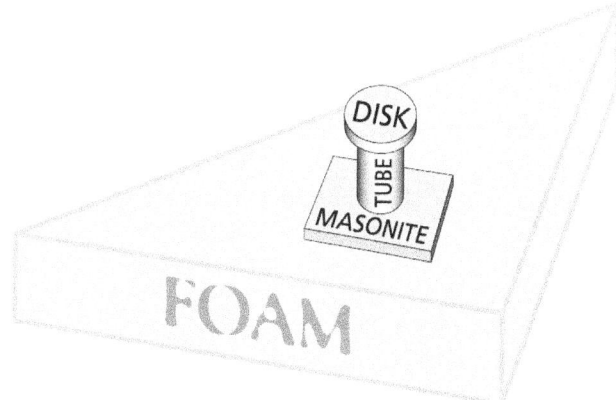

CHAPTER 12
Storytelling with Giant Tangrams
Illustrating stories with geometric shapes

Grades:	3–12
Time:	30–60 minutes
Math Concepts:	Geometry, spatial relations
Dance Concepts:	Dance with props, visual story-telling, shapes in space
Group size:	4-7
Space:	Requires clear floor
Materials:	One large tangram set per group (see instructions on page 109)
	Optional: pencil and paper, small tangram sets, ruler
Prerequisites:	*Moving with Giant Tangrams* (summarized in 12-1 below)
Related Activities:	*Stick Figures* also involves moving with large props

From ancient cave paintings to modern picture books, people have always used pictures to help tell stories. The pictures do not have to be complicated. For instance, the picture book "Grandfather Tang" weaves a tale about the invention of tangrams through pictures that are made of the seven simple tangram shapes.

In this activity groups of students make pictures with giant tangram shapes to illustrate stories they make up. This is a rich and exciting activity, requiring a great deal of creativity. To form the pictures, students must work together to solve complex spatial problems. To move from picture to picture, students must learn to move props with clarity and intention.

This activity grew directly out of our own creative work. We were fond of tangrams, and wanted to find a way to put them on stage. So we made a large set of tangrams out of cardboard and

attached handles. We found that if we held pieces from the back and kept the flat faces pointed away from us, the audience would see a living tangram set that changes magically from one shape to another. When we gave our giant tangram set to students, we were amazed and tickled by what children and adults created in a short amount of time.

12–1 Warm-up (5-10 minutes)

This requires several sets of giant tangrams. See page 109 for instructions. Before students tell stories, they need to learn how to move while holding giant tangrams. If the class has only 10-15 minutes, then try working through the main activities in the chapter *Moving with Giant Tangrams*. If there is less time, here are the important warm-up activities to try.
- Clear the space by pushing desks to the side of the classroom. Or move the class to a gym or other large space. Give each person one tangram piece. Have students stand in two lines facing each other, so they can see each other's shapes more clearly. Be sure students stand far enough apart that they will

not poke each other with pieces. For each of the following exercises, have half the class move while the other half watches. Then reverse: the other half moves while the first half watches. After everyone has tried moving, ask students to talk about what they saw that did or did not work.

- Solo movement: "Hold your shape in one hand, move it around slowly without moving your feet. Raise as high as you can, as low as you can, in front of your neighbor to the left, in front of your neighbor to the right. Twirl your shape by the handle. Try moving it so the front face stays flat in a plane, as if you were washing a big window, with the handle side toward you. This is how you usually want to hold the tangrams when you are performing for an audience."
- Movement in pairs: "Find a partner and stand side by side. One of you will be the freezer and the other person be the mover. Freezer, hold your piece still. Mover, slowly move your piece until it joins the freezer's piece to make a shape. Now switch roles. The person who was moving now hold your piece still. The person who was still now move your piece slowly until it joins the other piece to make a different shape. Take turns moving your pieces to make different shapes. Only one person should move at a time."
- Movement in groups: "Get in groups of seven, each group holding a complete tangram set. Make a shape with all pieces in your group. Try not to stand in front of your tangrams, so the audience can see the shapes. Make the widest shape you can. The tallest. The most compact. Make a shape with a hole in it. Make a square using some or all the pieces."

12–2 Storytelling (15-45 minutes)

In this activity, students create and perform a story illustrated with giant tangram shapes. This is a richly creative activity, touching on storytelling, geometry, theater, dance and group cooperation.

- Ask students to get in groups of seven. Each group gets a complete set of tangram pieces, one piece per person. If necessary, one person can handle two pieces. Younger students can work in smaller groups with fewer pieces — see section12-8 for shapes made with fewer than seven pieces.

There are two ways to proceed from here.

- **Story**. Hand out a page to each group showing different tangrams figures. Ask each group to choose three or more tangram figures that illustrate a story. For younger children it may be wise to limit the sequence to just two shapes. See section 12-7 for a handout with sample tangram shapes. Warning: the candlestick is extremely popular, so it may be good to encourage groups not to use it. Some groups may want to invent their own shapes to fit their stories. Have groups practice making their series of shapes with their pieces as they tell the story, until they can move from shape to shape smoothly and without hesitation. Challenge students to make shapes "in the air," so they are not resting on the floor.
- **Pure movement**. Alternatively, let students play with and manipulate the tangrams without regard to a literal story. Students should look for an interesting progression of shapes and transitions between shapes that forms a satisfying whole. Here are some questions to prompt exploration: "How does the progression start? What happens next? Do you do what is expected or break the pattern? What interesting effects can you create when all the shapes move?"

Ask each group to perform their story or sequence for the rest of the class. It helps if everyone else sits down while a group is performing. Optionally, ask the class to figure out a way to combine all the stories and sequences into one big story.

There are many interesting ways to use tangrams to tell stories. We encourage students to be creative. As a teacher keep your eyes open for fun and interesting things. Here are some of the many ideas we have seen.
- One person narrates the story, or everyone might take turns.
- Add vocal sound effects.
- Drop the shapes on the floor at the end.
- Create two completely separate shapes.
- Vibrate or waving the tangram pieces.
- Include your body as part of a shape.
- Use the handle on the back to make an eye for a creature.
- Animate a figure, for instance make the legs walk.

12–3 Sample Stories

This exercise unleashes surprising amounts of creativity. Writing teachers have found that giving students pictures to write about is an excellent way to get creative juices flowing. We have found that this is even more true with groups of students — groups typically invent their stories in only a few minutes.

For instance, fifth grade teacher Cathy Welch, teaching in Lakeport, California, tried tangram storytelling with her class of 30 students in a single 50-minute period. The class divided into four groups of approximately seven. Each group came up with a story. Stories were typically short and somewhat stream of consciousness. Here were the stories her class invented:
- A **ship** sailed out to sea and came across many **fish** and **birds**, then sailed on.
- A **sea dragon** lived in the **ocean** and ate **ships** and lived happily ever after.
- A **boat** sailed to sea but caught **fire** and burned up.
- There was a daring **pilot** who flew his **plane** everywhere and could land anywhere and that made him happy.

Once the groups had performed their stories, Cathy asked her students to make up a longer story linking all the group stories. The class voted on several suggestions. The winning entry was:
- A **pilot** lands on the **ship**, which then bumps into a **sea-dragon**, which it fights off. However the **ship** catches fire, and explodes into **flames** anyway.

This sequence required the group making the boat to remain on stage the entire performance, with the plane landing and turning into the pilot. The sea-monster tangrams attacked the ship, then withdrew off-stage. At the end, the ship collapsed into a heap of students and tangrams on the floor.

In other classrooms we have seen groups attempt to act out
- Existing stories, such as Cinderella, using figures like a **glass slipper**
- Nursery rhymes, like Jack be Nimble, using figures like a **candlestick**
- Current events. For instance the day after a plane crash teachers in a workshop we gave wanted to act out the disaster.
- Scenes from popular movies or TV shows
- Topics from class

12–4 Reflections and Assessment

The Dance

Once students have performed their tangram stories for each other in class, they may want to perform their stories outside the classroom. Performing is a great way to solidify an experience, raise the students' level of commitment, and deepen their understanding of what they did. Performing is also a great way to show student work to larger community, for instance at a school assembly or PTA event. Here are some tips for turning a classroom exercise into a public performance. For more ideas, see the chapter *Staging a Show*.

- **Clarity.** Learn to move as a group from shape to shape smoothly without talking to each other. Keep the focus on the shapes. Remember that the goal is to draw the audience's eyes to the shapes, not the performers.
- **Transitions.** The transitions from one shape to another are a big element of tangram stories. Also important is the order in which pieces come together and are pulled apart. Find transitions that help you tell the story best. Sometimes pieces may need to be handed off from one person to another. Consider how performers enter and exit the space.

- **Story.** Make sure the story has a clear beginning and end. To find a beginning, answer the question "How is the first shape formed?" or "How does the story begin?"
- **Rehearsal.** Rehearse, and get other people at the rehearsal to say what works and what does not work about the performance.
- **Staging.** A little attention to staging goes a long way. Wear simple solid coordinated colors. Add appropriate music. Light the performance area so it is brighter than the audience. Remove or hide distracting background. Be sure the audience is seated so they can see the performance. If students can perform on a raised stage, all the better — it might be possible to get technical help from someone who works with the stage or theater. For more ideas, see Chapter 13, *Staging a Show*.

The Mathematics

Creating a tangram story requires a good deal of mathematical problem solving. Here are some of the issues to raise in class discussion.

- **Plan.** "How did you plan your figures? Did you work with small tangrams first? Did you plan on the floor, or work directly in the air? Which was easier and why? How did you figure out how to move from one shape to another?"
- **Problem solving.** "What problems did you run into when making the figures with the giant tangrams? Did you have to modify any of the figures to make them easier to form? Did you have to change who was holding which piece in order to make the transitions work better? Did you run into any problems with the parallelogram – did you have to turn it around or reverse a figure?"
- **Record.** Ask groups to record their stories on paper, using a combination of words and diagrams. Translating a kinetic experience into static drawings is not easy! "Be sure to record not only which shapes you made and what was said, but also who was holding which piece and how people moved from shape to shape. Can you come back to your record several days later and reconstruct what you did? Can another group reconstruct your tangram story from your record?"

12–5 Further Activities

Here are other activities that involve storytelling with shapes.

Storytelling with other shapes. Use giant shapes other than tangrams to tell a story. For instance use pattern blocks, large squares, or circular hoops. Simple objects are fine; we know a choreographer (Ellen Sevy) who made a stunning piece in which dancers do nothing more than move large towels around. First find what interesting figures can be made with the shapes, then tell a story using some of those figures. See section 12-8 for shapes that go beyond tangrams.

Storytelling with bodies. Have students use their bodies to make large shapes. For instance, can they make a large face using four people to make the eyes, nose and mouth? What other large shapes can they make? Can they tell a story with these body shapes?

Make a book. Turn the tangram stories intoa picture books by drawing each figure on a separate page and adding words. Look at other tangram story books for inspiration.

12-6. Resources

Ford, Barbara E. *The Master Revealed-A Journey with Tangrams*, Tandoras's Box Press, 1990. A parable and many original figures, by the tangram-mistress herself.
http://www.illuminated.com/JH•ArtArchive/PageMill•Pages/FordPage.html

Lehet, John L. *A Sage's Journey, The Story of Tangrams*, Mathmaverick Press, 1998. A sage tells about his adventures. Illustrated with tangram figures.

Tompert, Ann. *Grandfather Tang's Story*, Crown Publisher, Inc., 1990. Picture story book about shape-changing foxes.

12-7. Sample Tangram Shapes

Here are some of the figures can be made with all seven tangram pieces. Copy this page and hand it out to your students as a starting point for their stories. Or hand out books of tangram shapes. Caution: if everyone gets the same handout, groups tend to tell similar stories, e.g. Jack be Nimble for the candlestick.

People. Make them walk and talk by moving pieces back and forth. Try changing arm and leg positions.

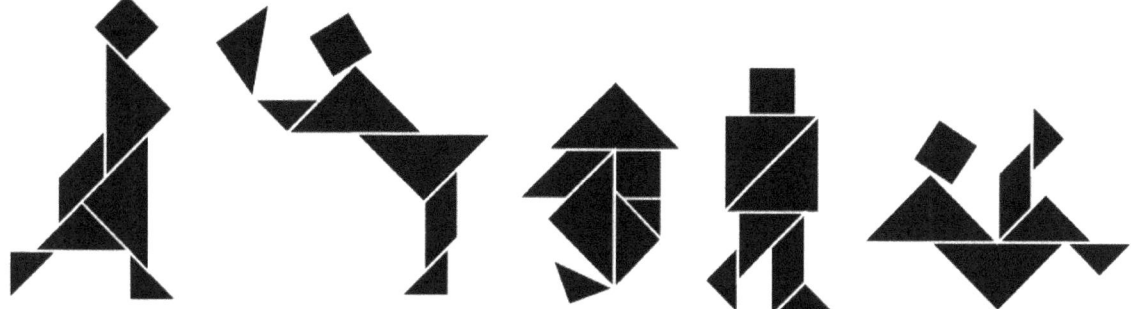

Animals. Try making the bird swim and the horse run. How else can the animals be animated?

Shapes. What ideas or objects might these shapes represent?

Things. What stories do these common objects suggest? Try making pairs of objects that go together.

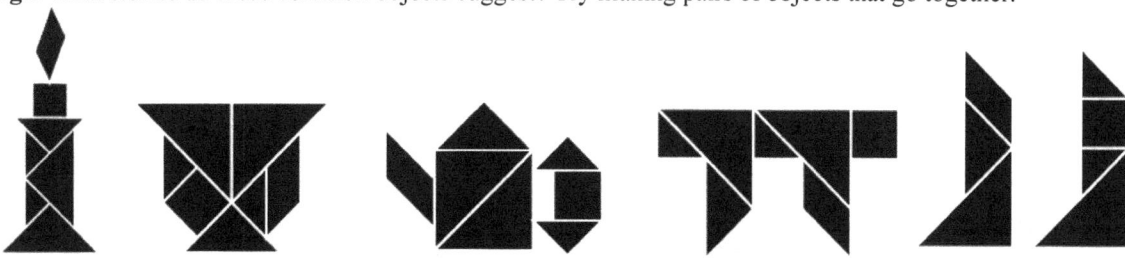

Settings. These figures are useful for putting the story in a particular setting.

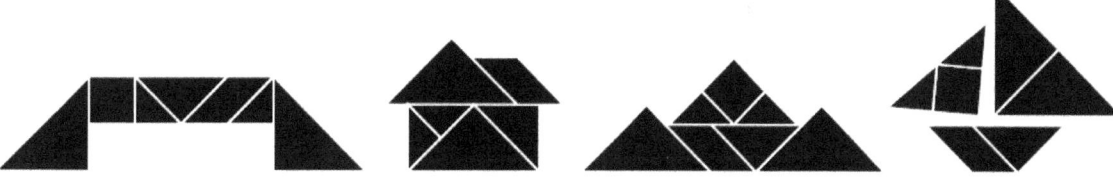

12-8. Beyond Traditional Tangrams

Groups may use fewer or more than seven pieces. They can arrange the tangram pieces in ways other than flat in a plane. Or make giant pieces that are completely different in shape from traditional tangrams.

Fewer pieces. Younger students work better with less than the full set of seven tangram pieces.

More pieces. The lion is made of two tangram sets. The chair and person are 7-piece figures that combine.

Other shapes. Here are two other tangram-like sets of shapes, one square, and one circular.

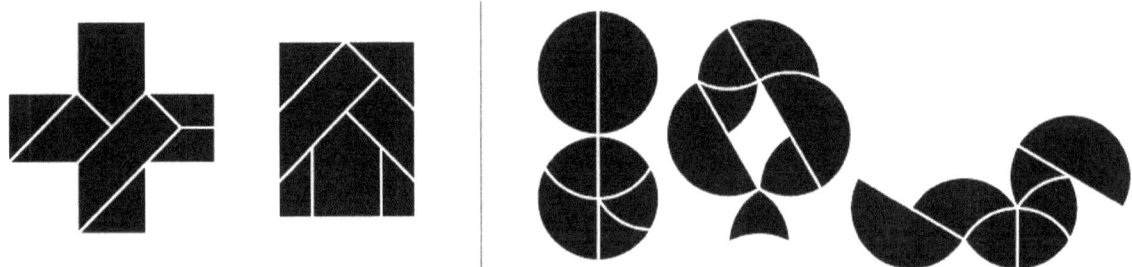

Other manipulatives. You can use classroom manipulatives like pattern blocks or pentominoes. Tetrominoes, shown here, are shapes made of four squares, from the popular computer game Tetris.

CHAPTER 13
Staging a Show
Creating a Mathematical Dance Performance

We designed every exercise in this book so it leads naturally to a dance performance or to a mathematical investigation. In this chapter we share some pointers on how to stage a mathematical dance show.

Once students have mastered a physical skill or composed a movement sequence, it is natural for them to want to share their enthusiasm by showing the dance to others. Preparing for a performance is excellent motivation for refining skills. Almost any exercise in this book, if practiced and refined, will create a performance.

Here are a number of reasons for staging a mathematical performance:
- Provides motivation for refining skills and deepening understanding.
- Brings the learning experience to a memorable and fitting close.
- Encourages students with skills in the arts to participate in mathematics, and those with mathematical skills to perform.
- Shares the work with parents, teachers, community members, and other students.
- Provides an opportunity for integrating mathematics and dance with history, writing, art, music, theater, and other subjects.
- May be a way to recruit students into school programs.

There are several levels of mathematical performance, from informal to highly prepared:
- **Showing work in class** immediately after the work has been produced.
- **A planned performance for another class** at a separate time from when the work was produced.
- **A planned performance to a larger group**, such as the school or local community, perhaps on a stage.

Here are tips for all three levels of performance.

13-1. Showing Work in Class

We often end a class period by having each group perform their creative work for the rest of the class. Here are some ideas to try:

Groups. Count off groups in advance so everyone knows when they will perform.

Performing space. Groups can take turns performing in the center of the space or at the front of the room. Or groups can perform where they are. In either case it helps if other groups sit down so everyone can see.

Staggered performance. Start with two groups in the center, the first group and the second group. The first group performs while the second group waits. When the first group is finished, they go back to their seats and the third group comes up to the center of the space while the second group performs. In general, each group comes to the center of the space when the previous group starts performing, so there are always two groups in the middle. This is a little tricky to explain, but it leads to a much smoother performance without pauses between groups.

Music. Playing music while groups perform makes the event feel more special. Students are often swept up by the music, and make their movements flow with it. Bring in tapes or CDs with music that has an appropriate pace for the exercise. Even though groups will not have rehearsed with the music, the eye tends to find relationships between the movements and the music.

Since many of the exercises require fairly slow and deliberate movements, relaxed classical music works well. Other exercises are more energetic. Some exercises, such as *Clap Your Name* (chapter 1) or *Storytelling with Giant Tangrams* (chapter 12), produce their own sounds and are best performed without music, or with non-metered music playing softly in the background. If teachers have musical skills or can bring in a musician, live music can be very exciting. A simple regular drumbeat can go a long way toward enlivening a classroom.

13-2. End of Term Performances

Students may want to plan a performance for a special event such as:
- The end of a unit.
- The end of a quarter or semester.
- A special day, such as a mathematician's birthday or Mathematics Education Month (April) or an arts emphasis week.

Preparing a performance takes work. Here are some pointers:

Staging. If a raised stage area is available, use it. Make sure the students are familiar with the stage area beforehand; this is a safety issue as well as a way to enhance and facilitate the performance. Be especially careful about any movements that take the performer near the edge of the stage or the wings. Make absolutely certain the stage is swept thoroughly and mopped before rehearsals and performances. Sharp objects, such as tacks, are common items that end up on school floors.

Seating. Can the audience see the performers? After working hard to make a dance which is enjoyable, the performers should be seen. If the audience is in chairs and the performers are on the same level as the audience (as in a cafeteria), anyone sitting behind the first few rows will have trouble seeing. An elevated stage is best, or, if the performance is for children, having the audience seated on the floor allows proper sight-lines.

Rehearsal. Give students time to rehearse their performance. It takes work to memorize a sequence of movements so it can be performed without fumbling or talking to each other. It is best if students can rehearse at least once in the same space in which they will perform.

Printed program. Preparing a printed program gives the event a feeling of being more official, and lets students take home something to show their families and friends. Enlisting student help to write, illustrate, print and handout the programs lets students participate in ways other than performing.

Announcer. Whether or not there is a printed program, it may be nice to have someone to announce each group. Groups may want to give themselves names, and title their work.

Costumes, sets. Costumes and sets can add character to the performance. Purchasing costumes is almost always unnecessary. Discuss with the students what they already have in their closets that might work. When dealing with props like the giant tangrams or PVC pipes, the shapes should stand out against the people, so wearing dark shirts and pants might help. Think about the color of the background of the performance space as well. The props can be painted other colors, including fluorescent colors. A large swatch of cloth or a poster might help as backdrop. Tables or chairs should be tested for sturdiness prior to anyone using them for dance work.

Lighting. In many classrooms it is possible to turn off some of the lights so only the performance area is lit. This helps the audience focus on the performance.

Entrances and exits. For a dance to begin on the correct foot, entrances need to be clear. Do students enter together? From the same or opposite sides? In a line? Some low and others high? Running or walking? Different choices have different effects; the important thing is that the choices have been made and agreed upon. The same questions may be asked about exits. Entrances and exits look better if there are wings which hide the areas off to the side of the stage from the audience. Though we tend to perform on formal stages with a crew to help, on occasion, when we perform in schools, we often improvise wings out of chalkboards, cafeteria tables, or bars draped with cloth.

13-3. Performances for Larger Groups

It may be of interest to stage a performance for a group larger than one class, such as:
- Other classes.
- School assemblies.
- School open house.
- Other schools.
- Community events or parades
- To accompany a science fair or other science-related school event.
- As part of a local library or community center program.

Staging public performances lets people outside the class see the results of the students' work. This could be good public relations for the class, the school, or for a mathematics program. Here are a few tips for performing for larger groups:

Bigger! In general, everything needs to be bigger. Movements need to be bigger to be seen. So do props. When groups rehearse, they should have one person looking at the performance from a distance, so to make sure performers are projecting adequately.

Louder! If there is speaking it needs to be done with a full voice, or amplification. Music may need to be amplified.

Coaching. Let students rehearse in the space in which they will perform. Have at least one person outside the group present who can watch from the audience's position and report on whether the performance "reads" well where the audience will be seated.

Technique. We have avoided recommending any particular dance technique. There are many wonderful forms of dance: modern dance, ballet, hip-hop, tap, square dance; we encourage students to draw on what they know. We are more interested in letting students participate at the level they are already comfortable with and develop from there. We find that having a clear intention in movement is actually more important than following a particular technical style...unless the goal is to master that technique. And we do not want teachers to feel that they must take dance classes before they can work with movement. Again, there is much that can be done with what students and teachers already know.

Critique. Are there distracting things in the performance that could be eliminated? Remember, everything the performers do is part of the performance: how they begin, how they end, what they say, where they are looking, how they move. In everyday life it is easy to ignore when people fidget or move unclearly; whereas on-stage everything is amplified, extra movements and shaky transitions become glaringly obvious. Give students time after any critique session to work on the problems. Try not to be too insistent: improvement and enjoyment are the goals, not perfection.

Sometimes it is easier for someone outside the performance to spot these distractions, especially if they are used to working on performances, so ask someone to watch the performance and give feedback. Or videotape a rehearsal and watch it. Or have someone in each group step out and critique the performance from time to time. Look for which movements come across clearly, and which do not. Learning to critique a performance is an important part of learning to dance.

Ensemble. Does the group move together? In sections where the group moves in unison, practice until everyone can move at the same time and in the same way. In the dance world this is called "ensemble". One way to get people to move together is to have them breath in unison at crucial points in the dance. Often people do not even realize they are doing a particular movement in different ways until someone watching points it out. However, in the attempt to be together, do not let the movements become smaller or tentative. In some ways, dancers moving slightly own of sync but with great energy are more fun to watch than those who are together because they are tentative and slow.

Record. Have each group record their on paper using pictures, words, and symbols, so they can remember what they did. Make a video record of the performance. Take photographs of the performers in costume or in interesting poses from the dances. Create a scrapbook or poster commemorating the performance.

Collaborate. Work with other teachers from dance, physical education, music, theater, art or English. Use their expertise and coaching in planning the performance.

Publicity. Publicize the performance. Simple black and white fliers made on a copy machine allow plenty of room for intriguing design. Public address announcements, notes in newsletters to parents, signs in front of the school, phone trees — the rule of thumb is that the potential audience needs to hear about the performance from more than one source.

Who does what? Although the performance may not demand a division of labor, students may enjoy taking responsibility for specific tasks. Discuss these in detail and make sure the lines of authority are clear. Examples:
- Tech Director. This may actually be someone from outside the class who is responsible for the audio/visual needs of the performance or the theater. Students may enjoy assisting in the technical work.
- Stage Manager. Oversees performers' entrances and exits, is responsible for movement of props and sets.
- House Manager. Determines when the audience will be seated, and sees to their needs (location of restrooms, special seating requirements).
- Publicist. Manages publicity for the show.
- Graphic Designer. Handles graphic work, flier layout, posters, program design.
- Costume Designer. Helps acquire, make, and manage costumes.

Program. Design an attractive program for the show, documenting who choreographed, performed in, or wrote text for each dance. Give music, costume, and set or prop construction credits. Include thanks to those who helped make the performance possible. Include the date and location of the performance so that the program becomes a memento of the event for the performers.

Handout. Create a handout explaining the mathematical ideas incorporated in the performance. Include graphics, further questions, references.

13-4. Other Mathematical Events

A mathematical stage performance is only one way to turn mathematics into a social or public event. Here are some other ideas, many of which we have actually tried:
- **Mathematical parties.** Party games, favors, food, invitations, activities.
- **Mathematical sports.** Give a familiar sport a mathematical twist. Try volleyball for three teams, invent new rules for ping pong, play baseball with five bases instead of four, soccer with two balls.
- **Many playground games**, like foursquare and tether ball, take place on geometric patterns. Draw a geometric pattern on the playground with duct tape or chalk and invent games to play on it.
- **Mathematical parade.** Incorporate mathematical floats, marching bands, drill teams, costumes. Get the local science museum to sponsor your classroom.
- **Mathematical drama.** Create a play about an event in the history of mathematics, or a way of using mathematics in the workday world.
- **Mathematical food contest.** Knotted bagels, edible polyhedra, tessellating cookies, cake decoration patterns. Play with your food. Eat your mathematics. Get local restaurants to participate.

CHAPTER 14
Assessment
Supporting students and building problem solving

Assessing math dance activities poses special challenges. Whenever we add new cross-disciplinary work to the curriculum, we need to find ways of determining how well students are doing with the material. This may seem a daunting task for teachers not experienced in all the relevant disciplines. Furthermore our math dance activities emphasize creative exploration, something not easily assessed with a multiple choice test.

In this chapter we give an overview of methods for assessing student performance in math dance activities. Teachers will need these methods to help them better understand the classroom work itself, as well as to help them guide the students. Each teacher will have to determine the best assessment methods for each situation. For more ideas on assessing particular activities, see the assessment and reflection section at the end of each chapter.

We believe that assessment should include much more than a determination of how well students did on a particular assignment. We agree with educators who feel that assessment should not only track their achievement, but provide feedback so they can continue to grow. It can also help us make decisions about what we do next in the classroom, as well as evaluate how overall school programs are doing.

In order to do all these things assessment cannot begin after the lesson. Educators must constantly be gathering information on what is happening in the classroom: watching and listening to students as they work, and making notes about what we see; asking questions that propel students to the next level; thinking about and talking with colleagues about the progress the students are making; collecting writings or drawings the students create while doing their work; responding to their performances critically but supportively.

For assessment to be effective, it must be flexible enough to accommodate the open-ended and exploratory nature of this work. Assessment methods such as multiple choice tests and paper and pencil calculations are not adequate for evaluating instruction that is student-centered and problem-oriented.

14-1. Assessment Standards

Much has been written about changing the nature of assessment in the classroom. For example, the National Council of Teachers of Mathematics has developed standards for assessing mathematics that go far beyond conventional tests. Though intended to apply to mathematics education, these standards are an excellent point of departure when looking at interdisciplinary work. They state that assessment should:
- Support learning and become an ongoing part of the learning process.
- Reflect the knowledge that all students need to know and be able to do.
- Promote equity.
- Be an open process. (Students should understand expectations and grading process.)
- Promote valid inferences about learning. (Often best accomplished via multiple measures of student success: journals, problems solved, projects, performance, for example).
- Be coherent. (The assessment process should reflect the kind of work the students were asked to do.)

Here are examples of how to follow several of these guidelines in classes integrating creative movement and mathematics:

Assessment should support learning and become an ongoing part of the learning process. For example, informal assessment that happens while students are working allows teachers to take notes on the work being done, and to note individual problems or accomplishments. When students work in groups the teacher may walk around the room observing without distracting the students. Follow-up questions are then easier to formulate. Many of our assignments encourage this kind of side-line observation by teachers.

For example, in chapter 1, when we observed students counting handshake patterns, we noticed a variety of sensible decisions about how to decide when two handshakes were different. Rather than interrupt and "correct" or further clarify the assignment directions, we allowed time at the end for a discussion. We made sure that competing interpretations of the directions were discussed, and this allowed students to use higher level thinking to examine the problem. It also lead us to alter the outcomes we expected from the class session to include discussion of how the students interpreted the assignment, and whether their counts were consistent with their interpretation.

Assessment should reflect the mathematics that all students need to know and be able to do. By the same token, it should reflect the dance and arts knowledge that students are expected to master. This book is in no way a complete mathematics or dance curriculum, and we are not outlining any particular collection of mathematics skills or dance styles that we expect teachers to build such a curriculum around. However our general approaches to dance and mathematics will be familiar to educators in either field. For example, we have advocated more emphasis on symmetry and transformational geometry, as opposed to memorization of geometry facts and practice with theorem and proof. Our methodologies and approaches to dance put us squarely in the realm known as "modern dance."

We feel that teachers should pay attention not only to procedural skills in mathematics (how to do multiplication, for example), but to how to use that knowledge in a problem solving situation. In the same way, particular dance styles or traditions (such as ballet or hip-hop) are important, but students should gain experience in learning how to solve choreographic or performance problems within whatever dance tradition they are studying. We expect that such problem-solving will involve identifiable mathematical and movement knowledge. For example, they must understand distinctions between types of symmetries, and might be asked to recognize how they are used in performances by professional dancers within a particular dance tradition.

Assessment should promote equity. One of the popular fallacies about mathematics is that some groups of people are more likely to "have a math mind," than others. Dance is also often seen as an activity for girls and not boys, at least within the larger American culture. Activities such as those in this book encourage wider participation in both disciplines.

Teachers should assess their students' success with the activities keeping these traditional barriers in mind. Thus a student who uses sports movement in solving one of the problems in this book, might be using ease in a competitive form of movement to open up to expressive movement, and should be encouraged to do so. A student who is normally restless in a traditional symbolically oriented math class, might find the kinesthetic and visual aspects of the work here freeing, Teachers who approach the math dance activities keeping in mind students' differences in experience, physical condition, gender, and ethnic, cultural, or social backgrounds, will be more able to find ways to encourage — and assess — all students fairly.

Assessment should be an open process. In the context of the math dance work, this means that students should understand in advance how any grading of their work will be done, and after the fact should see how criteria were applied. For example, students might be expected to finish a day's activities with a performance of a movement phrase which tells a story with the giant tangrams, and also complete a written or drawn description of their work. Let them know what is expected of their paperwork, whether it is to be handed in (or perhaps displayed on a bulletin board), and whether they should plan to perform their story to the rest of the class.

An alternative to product-oriented grading is that of "rubrics." In a rubric, points are given according to a pre-established set of criteria. For example,
- 0 points for no work or off-task work
- 1 point for some understanding and accomplishment
- 2 points for diligent work that does not yet meet the goals of the assignment
- 3 points for work that meets or surpasses the goals.

Much has been written about rubrics elsewhere; consult the references at the end of this chapter.

14-2. Assessment Questions

Assessing dance. Here are some general questions to ask in evaluating the dance work of students:
- Did the clarity of the movement increase with practice?
- Did the dance phrase include the ideas we were working with?
- Did the students commit to creating and working on the dances?
- Did the students perform or were they hesitant or afraid?
- Did the work display inventiveness and variety?
- Were the students moving together?
- Did they participate in critiquing the other work of the students? (If critiquing seems difficult for students, it might be worthwhile to try to facilitate the discussion by asking leading questions.)
- Were the comments constructive and usable in some way?
- Did their comments on student work refer to the work, or did it become personal?
- If the activity involved the students in creating a written or hand drawn description of their movement work, did others try to use it to reconstruct the dance, and how well did that work?

Assessing mathematics. Similar questions can be asked about open-ended mathematics work. In addition, here are some other useful questions that apply specifically to mathematical performance.
- Does the student use mathematical vocabulary properly? Is the student able to name mathematical concepts when they occur?
- Can the student explain the problem accurately? Is the solution consistent with the interpretation of the problem, even if the interpretation is different from what was intended?
- Can the student explain the reasoning behind a solution through writing and pictures?
- Can the student generalize and extend the mathematical ideas in a creative and logical manner?
- Can the student relate the math dance activities to concepts from the mathematical curriculum?

Of course many of these are relative questions. The more carefully the we look at the students' work, the better we can discern progress.

14-3. Reflection

The kind of open-ended assignments that we have included demand a lot of critical thinking and self-examination. How we ask questions, as well as the facts addressed by the questions, can determine how much learning and growth will take place.

Reflecting on dance. Encourage the class to watch whenever others are performing. Here are some questions that help students develop "aesthetic valuing" — the ability to make distinctions and aesthetic choices about movement expression.
- "What did you notice in the other groups?"
- "What did you learn from what you saw?"
- "What worked well? What did not?"
- "Did the work performed have a clear beginning and ending?"
- "Was there a sense of development, or did it remain in the same framework most of the time?"
- "Did some dances have a quality or theme to them?" (Sometimes these might appear without the conscious intent of the students creating the work.)
- "What feelings did the movement/phrase/dance evoke?"
- "If you liked something can you figure out why?"
- "Can you think of how the dancers could still work on the performance work you liked?"
- "Find words to describe your favorite dance."
- "What seemed out of place in a dance? Why does it seem out of place? "
- "Brainstorm on ways to change/enhance/improve what you or your group performed."

Reflecting on mathematics. Here are some suggestions on how to ask mathematical questions.

- Ask questions that elicit a variety of responses and ideas from students, not just "the right answer."
- It is all right to ask questions which do not seem to include enough information. This develops the students' ability to clarify their interpretations of a given problem. Then they must find answers consistent with their interpretations. (This applies to dance too, but in a more qualitative manner.)
- Utilize a variety of writing assignments: ask them to write a letter to a friend or relative explaining the mathematical ideas in the work they did. Or write an advertisement doing the same thing. Or draw and write text for a cartoon. Or write a short story or play.
- Utilize journals, "instant writing" (everything is written down without forethought), or questionnaires.
- Have the students interview each other about the work, and record the results.
- Occasionally ask questions that go beyond the understandings inherent in the work they have done, to get them thinking about "the next level."
- Ask for comparisons of these ideas with things they have learned about in other subjects. For example, "You have studied symmetry in dance and mathematics. Can you think of appearances of symmetry in politics?"
- Ask "overview" questions that ask the students to place new knowledge in a larger perspective. (For example, "How is symmetry really used in dance?)

14-3. Resources

Kulm, G. *Mathematics Assessment: What Works in the Classroom.* San Francisco: Jossey-Bass, 1994. Models and ideas about assessment for the classroom.

Lambdin, Diana V., Paul E. Kehle, Ronald V. Preston (Eds.). *Emphasis on Assessment: Readings from NCTM's School-Based Journals.* Reston, VA: National Council of Teachers of Mathematics, 1996. 30 articles from NCTM journals on assessment, along with an annotated bibliography.

National Council of Teachers of Mathematics. *Assessment Standards for School Mathematics.* Reston, Virginia, 1995. The most recent document by the major math education organization in the United States.

Stenmark, Jean Kerr, (Ed.). *Mathematics Assessment: Myths, Models, Good Questions, and Practical Suggestions.* Reston, VA: National Council of Teachers of Mathematics, 1991. New directions in assessment, with plenty of examples.

http://www.nfer.ac.uk/summary/eaj.htm. Arts Education in Secondary School: Effects and Effectiveness. This report presents the results of an important three-year study of the effectiveness of arts education in English and Welsh secondary schools.

Mathematics and Dance Bibliography

We often get requests from students and researchers looking for information on mathematics and dance. Unfortunately, not much has been published on these subjects, and so we hope that this working bibliography may help point interested people to helpful sources.

Some items are included even though we do not currently have complete bibliographic information for them, and some of the sources we have only seen referenced in other works. We would greatly appreciate any additional references or missing information; please send these to schafferkarl@fhda.edu. These references were compiled during 1997-2001, and included visits to the Lincoln Center Library for the Performing Arts in New York City, and the Laban Center library, also in New York. The Lincoln Library classifications are included, where known, to simplify access to those references.

For those unfamiliar with dance and dance notation, a number of the references relate to the work of Rudolf Laban, and his followers. Laban developed the most commonly used dance notation, Labanotation, based on a very scientific analysis of human movement.

At the end we will soon include our dances which include significant mathematical ideas or inspiration. We would appreciate any information on dances or performances readers know about with strong connections to mathematics.

References

Andrews, Angela Giglia. "Developing Spatial Sense — a Moving Experience," *Teaching Children Mathematics,* Jan., 1996, pp 290-293. Reston, Va.: National Council of Teachers of Mathematics. Activities which help young children develop spatial ability.

Arnold, Eric B., and Frances Trix. English Country Dance as a Living Tradition Viewed Through Symmetry and Symmetry Breaking. Lincoln Library.

Bartenieff, Irmgaard, with Dori Lewis. *Body Movement — Coping with the Environment,.* New York: Gordon and Breach Science Publishers, 1980 and 1988.

Blank, Carla, and Jody Roberts. *Live on Stage: Performing Arts for Middle School Teacher Resource Book.* Palo Alto: Dale Seymour Publications, 1997. Projects and activities that present a cross-disciplinary approach to teaching the performing arts,

Bradley, Elizabeth (elizabeth.bradley@colorado.edu), David Capps, and Andee Rubin. "Can Computers Learn to Dance?" *Proceedings of International Dance and Technology.* Tempe, AZ 1999. The use of computer programs in the analysis and creation of dance sequences. See www.cs.colorado.edu/lizb/chaotic-dance.html.

Bradley, Elizabeth (elizabeth.bradley@colorado.edu), and Joshua Stuart. "Using Chaos to Generate Choreographic Variations," *Proceedings of the Fourth Experimental Chaos Conference*, Aug. 1997, Boca Raton. Describes a method for using chaos theory to create variations on dance sequences. See www.cs.colorado.edu/lizb/chaotic-dance.html.

Bradley, Elizabeth (elizabeth.bradley@colorado.edu), and Joshua Stuart. "Using chaos to generate variations on movement sequences," *Chaos*, Vol. 8, No. 4, Dec. 1998. The use of chaos theory in creating and altering dance sequences.See www.cs.colorado.edu/lizb/chaotic-dance.html.

Brown, A.K., and M. Parker, *Dance Notation for Beginners*. London: Dance Books, 1984.

California State Board of Education. *Visual and Performing Arts Framework for California Public Schools, Kindergarten Through Grade Twelve.* Sacramento: California Department of Education, 1996. California's state framework for arts education.

California State Board of Education. *Challenge Standards for Student Success, Visual and Performing Arts.* Sacramento: California Department of Education, 1998. California's arts standards.

Clements, Douglas H. and Michael T. Battista. *Geometry and Spatial Reasoning*, in *Handbook of Research on Mathematics Teaching and Learning,* edited by Douglas A. Grouws., pp420-464. New York: Simon & Schuster Macmillan, 1992. A scholarly overview of current knowledge on geometric and spatial reasoning.

Cook, Wayne D. *Center Stage: A Curriculum for the Performing Arts.* Palo Alto: Dale Seymour Publications, 1993. A grades 4-6 performing arts curriculum.

Del Grande, John, and Lorna Morrow, with Douglas Clements, John Firkins, Jeane Joyner. "Geometry and Spatial Sense," *Curriculum and Evaluation Standards for School Mathematics Addenda Series, Grades K-6.* Reston, Va.: National Council of Teachers of Mathematics, 1993. Includes some physical exercises for mathematical explorations.

Dell, Cecily. *A Primer for Movement Description: Using Effori-Shape and Supplementary Concepts.* New York: Dance Notation bureau Press, 1977. Presents the system of effort-shape, a scientific system based on Rudolf Laban's work, which is used to analyze dance and movement.

Dennison, Paul E. and Gail E. Dennison. *Brain Gym, Teachers Edition,* Revised. Ventura, CA: Edu-Kinesthetics, Inc., 1994. A series of exercises put together by the Dennisons in efforts to deal with Paul Dennison's dyslexia and visual problems, and incorporating work in curriculum development and psychology.

Flatishhler, Reinhard. *The Forgotten Power of Rhythm.* Mendocino, CA: LifeRhythm, 1992. Essay on the use of rhythm in world music.

Gardner, Howard, *Frames of Mind, The Theory of Multiple Intelligences,* New York: Harper Collins, Basic Books, 1985. Lays out the theories of multiple intelligence, including the kinesthetic.

Gilbert, Anne Green. *Teaching the Three R's Through Movement Experiences, A Handbook for Teachers,* see section on Mathematics, pp83-146. First published by Burgess Publishing Company in 1977, republished by Prentice-Hall, Inc. Available from www.creativedance.org. Many, many ideas for movement activities, somewhat oriented toward primary grades, but adaptable to others.

Greeley, Nansee, and Theresa Reardon Offerman. "Now & Then, Dancing in Time and Space," *Mathematics Teaching in the Middle School,* Vol. 4, No. 3, Nov.-Dec. 1998, pp 192-199. Reston, Va.: National Council of Teachers of Mathematics. Having a mathematical background could be helpful to the teaching of dance and drama.

Guest, Ann Hutchinson, *Dance Notation: The process of recording movement on paper,* New York: Dance Horizons, 1984.

Herbison-Evans, Don. "Symmetry in Dance." Imprint, Technical Report 329, Basser Department of Computer Science, University of Sydney, Australia. (8 pages). Philosophical overview of symmetry in dance. (Lincoln Center Library, don@socs.uts.edu.au).

Hall-Marriot, Natalie Louise (nataliem@mosaix.com.au), and Don Herbison-Evans (don@socs.uts.edu.au). "A Computer Interpreter of Classical Ballet Terminology." Imprint, Technical Report TR264, Basser Department of Computer Science, University of Sydney, Australia. Description of a project to develop a classical ballet interpreter to turn the written language of ballet into computer animations of the ballet.

Hanna, Judith Lynne. *Partnering Dance and Education: Intelligent Moves for Changing Times..* Champagne, Illinois: Human Kinetics, 1999. Examines trends and issues in dance education, while arguing for inclusion of dance in public education.

Hannaford, Carla. *Smart Moves: Why Learning Is Not All in Your Head.* Alington, VA: Great Ocean Publishers, 1995. The role of the human body in learning and thinking, presented in a scientific and readabe manner. She discusses the Brain Gym activities of Paul and Gail Dennison.

Herbison-Evans, Don (don@socs.uts.edu.au). "Dance and the Computer: A Potential for Graphic Synergy." Imprint, Technical Report 422, Basser Department of Computer Science, University of Sydney, Australia. (5 pages). (Lincoln Center Library).

Holt, Michael, and Zoltan Dienes.*Let's Play Math.* New York: Walker Publishing Company, 1973. Includes a chapter on movement activities for dance, for younger children (ages 5 to 7 approximately.)

Hughes, Lanston. *The book of Rhythms.* New York: Oxford University Press, 1995. Originally published as *The first book of rhythms*, New York: F. Watts, 1954. A delightful exploration of rhythm in language, art and life, and a good source for movement ideas.

Humphrey, Doris. *The Art of Making Dances.* New York Grove Press, 1959. Contains the proclamation that "symmetry is boring!". By this she seems to mean mirror symmetry. Humphrey was one of the seminal figures in Modern Dance and this book is a compendium of her craft.

Jamison, Robert E. "Rhythm and Pattern: Discrete Mathematics with an Artistic Connection for Elementary School Teachers," *Discrete Mathematics in the Schools,* ed. by Rosenstein, Joseph G., Deborah S. Franzblau, Fred.S. Roberts. DIMACS Series in Discrete Mathematics and Theoretical Compute Science, Vol. 36., published by the American Mathematical Society, 1997, pp203-222. An overview of how symmetry activities and the arts may be used in teaching mathematics. Movement ideas inspired by the movement form eurythmy, taught in the Waldorf Schools.

Jensen, Eric. *Teaching with the Brain in Mind.* Alexandria, VA: Association for Supervision and Curriculum Development, 1998. Integrates latest research on learning and the brain with techniques for the classroom. See chapter 9 Movement and Learning.

Julesz, B. *Foundations of Cyclopean Perception,* Chicago Univ. of Chicago Press, 1971, pg57. Referenced in Herbison-Evans, contains data on studies showing human abilities to perceive various kinds of symmetries.

Kaproff, Jay. *Connections: The Geometric Bridge between Art and Science.* New York: McGraw-Hill, Inc.1991. A wide-ranging introduction to pattern and design in art and science.

Kluger-Bell, Barry, and the School in the Exploratorium. *The Exploratorium Guide to Scale and Structure: Activities for the Elementary Classroom.* Portsmouth, NH: Heinemann, 1995. "Body Balance," pp 97-99 has students explore with a partner the way bodies balance. The book compiles activities for the classroom that involve building and scale.

de Laban, Juana. Dance Index, Vol. 5, No. 4, 1946, referenced in Thie, gives a description of a number of dance notations from ancient to present.

Lakoff, George, and Rafael E. Núñez. *Where Mathematics Comes From, How the Embodied Mind Brings Mathematics Into Being.* New York: Basic Books, 2000. A philosophical treatise on how mathematical ideas originate in everyday bodily experience.

Lambdin, Diana V., and Dolly Lambdin. "Connecting Mathematics and Physical Education through Spatial Awareness," *Connecting Mathematics across the Curriculum,* 1995 Yearbook of the National Council of Teachers of Mathematics, edited by Peggy A. House and Arthur F. Coxford, pp. 147-151. Reston Va.: NCTM, 1995. Espouses mathematical explorations in physical education.

Longstaff, Jeffrey Scott. *Moving in Crystals: A Continued Integration of Polyhedral Geometry with Rudolf Laban's Choreutics, Towards its Use as a Choreographic Tool,* Master of Science Thesis for Department of Dance and the Graduate School, Univ. of Oregon, June, 1988. (Laban Center Library, New York).

Maletic, Vera. *Body – Space – Expression, The Development of Rudolf Laban's Movement and Dance Concepts,* New York: Moton de Gruyter, 1987. Theoretical underpinnings of Laban's work.

Milligan, J.G. *Won't You Join the Dance,* Paterson, London, 1976, pg 11. referenced in Herbison-Evans, with respect to symmetry in Scottish dance.

National Council of Teachers of Mathematics (NCTM), *Curriculum and Evaluation Standards for School Mathematics,* Reston, Va.: NCTM, 1989, revised in 2000. The reform standards for mathematics teaching, which include copious suggestions that mathematics education be more closely tied to human activites.

Peterson, Ivars. "Dancing Chaos," *Ivars Peterson's Math Trek,* online column at www.maa.org, Jan. 11, 1999. Wash. D.C.: Mathematical Association of America. An account of the use of chaos theory to generate movement sequences. See also articles by Bradley, et al.

Phillips, Richard. "Jumping at Mathematics," Micromath, Summer 1989, pp 37-39. Complete reference temporarily lost. Describes the use of electronic mats which count the number of steps taken on them for classroom math activities.

Piaget, Jean, and Bärbel Inhelder. *The Child's Conception of Space.* Translated by F. J. Langdon and J. L. Lunzer. New York: W.W. Norton and Company, 1967. First published in France in 1948. The groundbreaking study of the development of spatial thinking in children.

Piaget, Jean, Bärbel Inhelder, and Alina Szeminska. *The Child's Conception of Geometry.* Translated by E.A. Lunzer. New York: W. W. Norton and Company, 1981, originally published in 1960 by Routland and Kegan Paul. The development of geometric measurement ability in children.

Rogers, Laurence. "A Surprising Sensor," *Micromath,* Summer 1989, pp 41-42. Complete reference temporarily lost. Describes the use of motion detectors in classroom math activities.

Salter, Alan. "Icosahedral Symmetry Operations: Spiraloid 12-ring surfaces and their derivatives," *The Laban Art of Movement Guild Magazine,* Nov. 1967, pp 13-19. Examines sequences along points of the Laban icosahedron from point of view of symmetry. Assumes knowledge of notation for these points. (*MGZA — Lincoln Center Library)

Salvadori, Mario. *The Art of Construction: Projects and Principles for Beginning Engineers and Architects..* Chicago: Chicago Review Press, 1990. Originally published as *Building: The Fight Against Gravity,* Atheneum, 1979. Contains many ideas for using the body to illustrate architectural and engineering principles.

Schmidt, R.A. *Motor Skills,.* New York: Harper and Row, 1975, pg 45. Referenced in Herbison-Evans, showing that motor skills improve with repetition, even after millions of repetions.

Shillinger, Joseph. "The Mathematical Basis of the Arts." Referenced in Thie, classified arts according to "length, breadth, height, time, and means of perception." Apparently most interested in music.

Siegel, Marcia. Math. "Mac, and the Music," *Dance Ink,* Vol 4, #2, Summer 1993, discussion of uses of computers in music and dance.

Slocum, Jerry, and Jack Bottermans, *The Book of Ingenious & Diabolical Puzzles,* New York: Random House, Times Books, 1994. Contains a short history of tangrams, and. This and other books by Slocum and Bottermans describe a variety of mathematical puzzles which may be made into entertaining dance props.

Stewart, Ian. "Dances with Dodecahedra," in Sep. 1999 *Scientific American,* Vol. 281, Number 3. Article about Karl Schaffer and Scott Kim's constructions of polyhedral string figures.

Thie, Joseph A. *Rhythm and Dance Mathematics,.* Minneapolis: published by Joseph Thie, 1964 (once available from the Dance Mart, Box 48, Brooklyn, NY 11229.) Applies the mathematical technique known as correlation analysis to sequences of dance steps. Includes some analysis of dance and mathematics with a larger scope. This book is available in the Lincoln Center Library and in the Dance Collection of the Birmingham Public Library, in Birmingham, Alabama.

Thurston, William P. "On Proof and Progress in Mathematics," *New Directions in the Philosophy of Mathematics: An Anthology.* Revised and Epanded Paperback Edition, ed. by Thomas Tymoczko, pp337-355. Princeton, New Jersey: Princeton University Press, 1998, originally published in 1986. Thurston has some interesting things to say about the role of kinesthetic experience in mathematical thinking.

Warkentin, Don R. "Finger Math in Geometry," *The Mathematics Teacher,* vol 93, No. 4, April 2000, pp 266-268. Reston, Va.: National Council of Teachers of Mathematics. The use of finger and hand gestures in the math classroom.

Wechsler, Robert. "Symmetry in Dance," *Contact Quarterly,* vol. 15, #3, Fall 1990, pp 29-33, Northhampton, MA. Examines various ways to use symmetry in choreography.

Wechsler, Robert A. *Analysis of 'Reversals' in the Cunningham Dance Technizue. Issues Concerning the Perception of Symmetry in Dance,,* in Lincoln Center Library collection. Contact: robert@palindrome.de

Yakimanskaya, I.S. *The Development of Spatial Thinking in Schoolchildren,* vol. 3 of Soviet Studies in Mathematics Education, translated by Robert H. Silverman. Reston, Virginia: National Council of Teachers of Mathematics, 1991. Originally published in 1980 by Pedagogika, Moscow, as *Razvitieprostranstvennogo myshlenlya shkol'nikov.* Scholarly work on the development of spatial thinking and its relationship to mathematics education.

About the Authors

Dr. Schaffer and Mr. Stern Dance Ensemble. From a dance comparing the extinction of the dinosaurs with the fate of jocks to a "reverent parody" of Hamlet, from vaudevillian handshakes to ancient Chinese stories of flying machines, the Ensemble, co-founded and co-directed by Karl Schaffer and Erik Stern, is known for its highly physical and often humorous choreography. Their performance, educational and written work integrating the worlds of mathematics and dance in surprising and groundbreaking ways anticipated the spread of arts integration methods. They have toured throughout North America and in Europe and Asia, most recently performing in Houston, Madison, Buffalo, Hungary, France, at the Museum of Mathematics in New York, and at the National Science Museum in Seoul, South Korea. The company has received five National Endowment for the Arts awards for their cross-disciplinary performance work and Schaffer and Stern are Kennedy Center for the Performing Arts Teaching Artists. Visit www.mathdance.org, and view their TEDx Manhattan Beach video.

Karl Schaffer is a dancer, choreographer, and mathematician. His concert *The Daughters of Hypatia* celebrating women mathematicians throughout history has toured nationally and his concert *Mosaic* deals with peace, justice and culture in the Mideast. He has performed and/or taught contemporary dance, tap, Tai Chi, Bharatya Natyam, Flamenco, and folk dance. He received a Ph.D. in mathematics from UC Santa Cruz and teaches math at De Anza College.

Erik Stern is a choreographer, dancer, musician and interdisciplinary educator. His work *Demolition Derby* brought together Alzheimer's organizations and corporations. His collaborative projects Pattern Play and DanceScienceFest are being presented nationally. A Professor of Dance at Weber State University in Ogden, Utah, he received his B.A. in Biology from UC Santa Cruz and an M.F.A in Dance from CalArts.

Scott Kim is a renowned mathematician, graphic artist, author, educator, and puzzle master. He wrote the monthly puzzle column in Discover Magazine for ten years, and his puzzles have appeared in Games Magazine, Scientific American, and numerous computer games. His book *Inversions* delves into symmetric play with letterforms, and Scott has been called "the M.C. Escher of letterforms." He currently designs games for abcmouse.com, has a Ph.D. in computer science from Stanford University, and lives in Burlingame, CA.